I0492093

# THIS BOOK BELONGS TO

_____

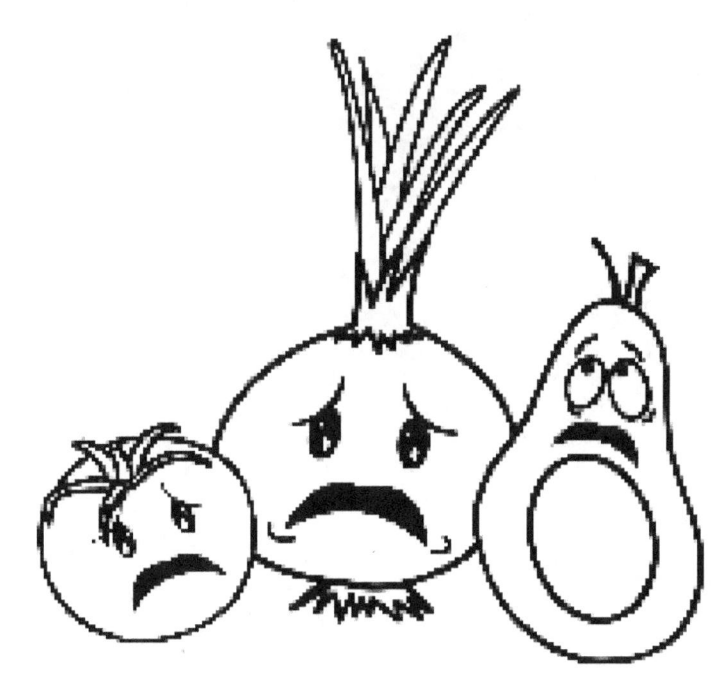

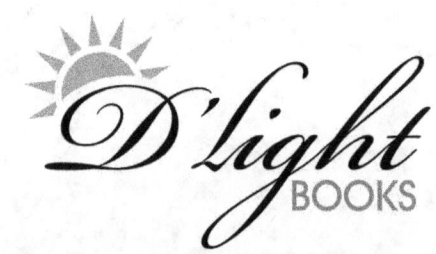

Copyright 2020 D'Light Books

WWW.DLIGHTBOOKS.COM

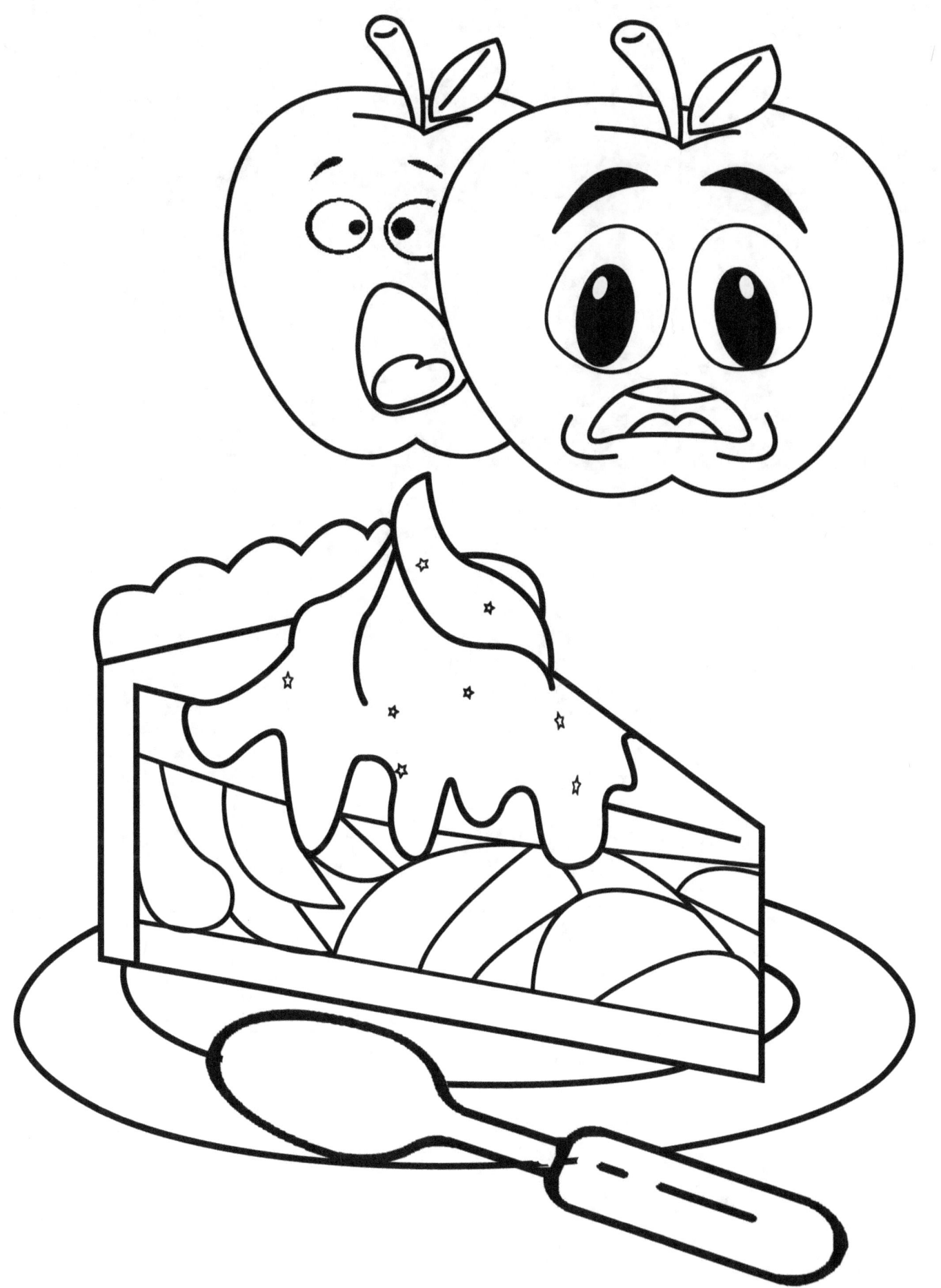

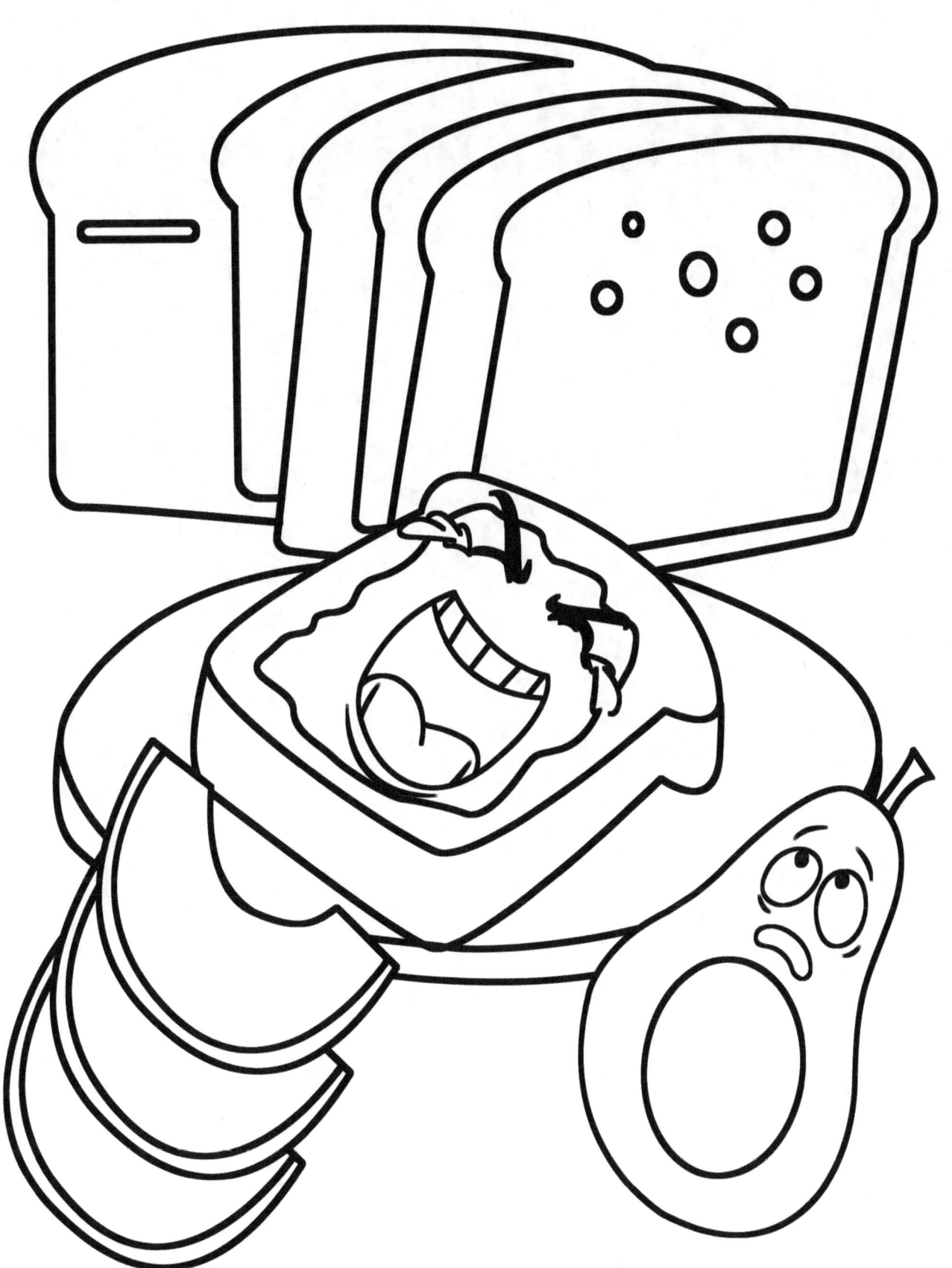

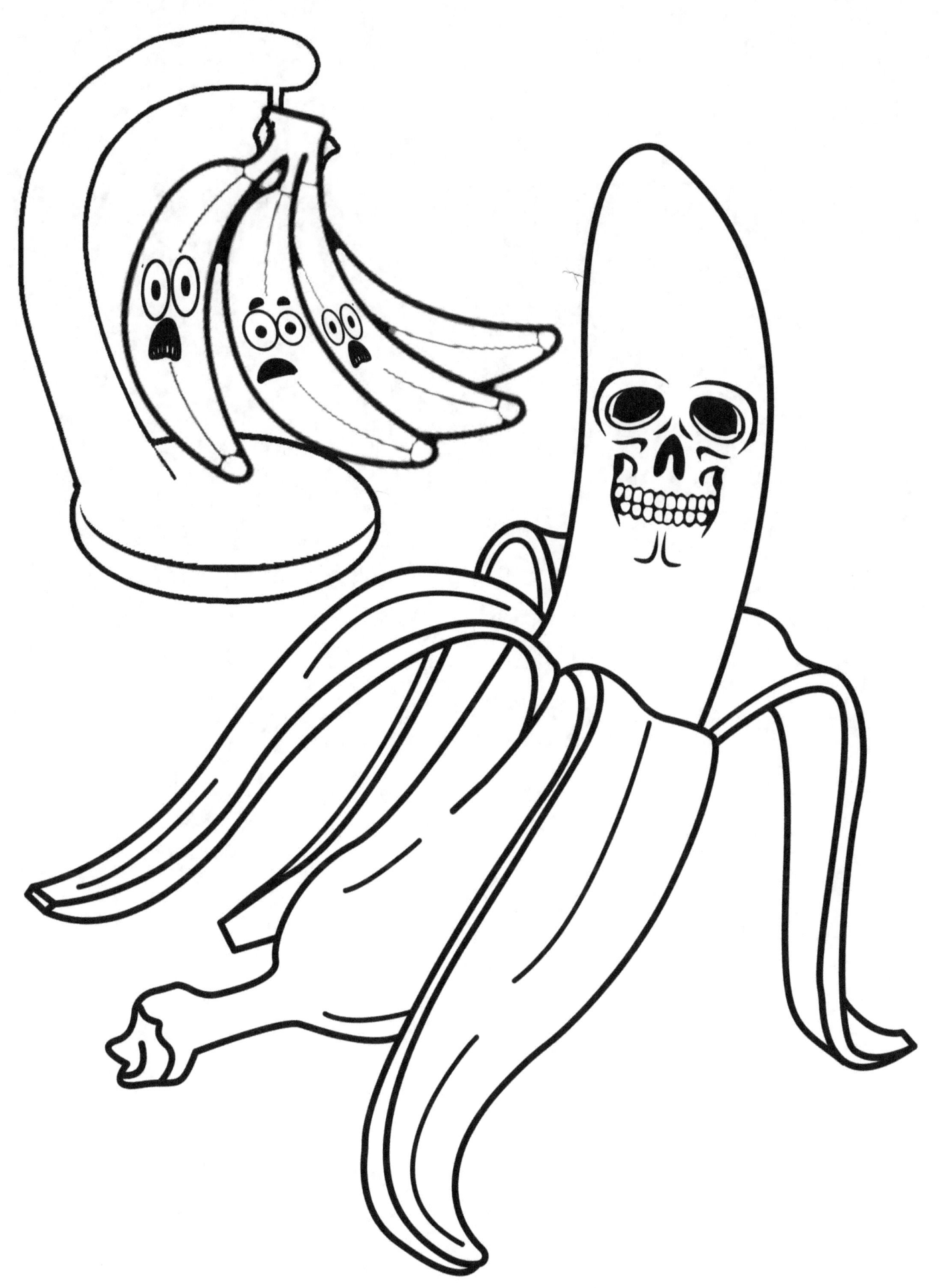

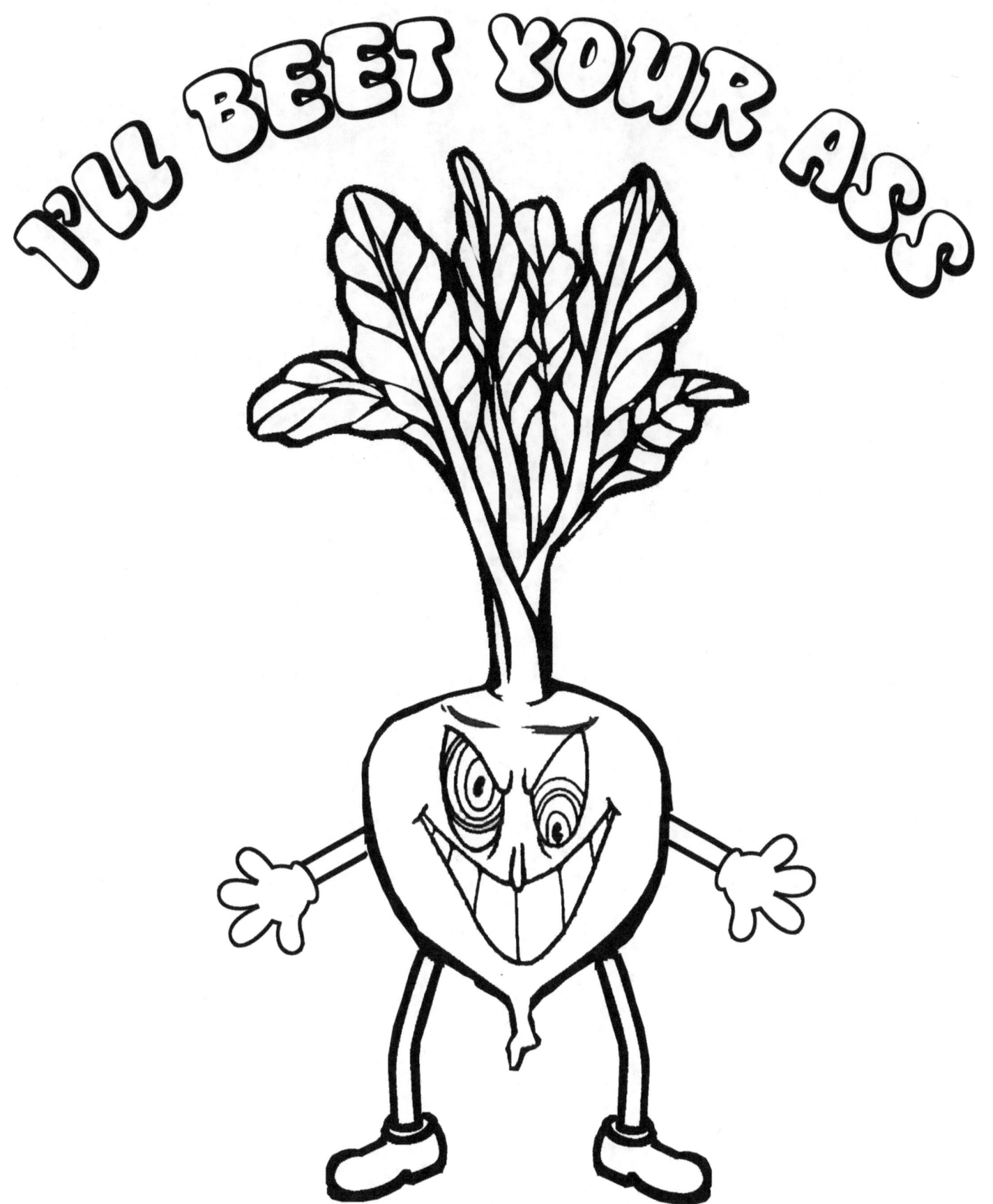

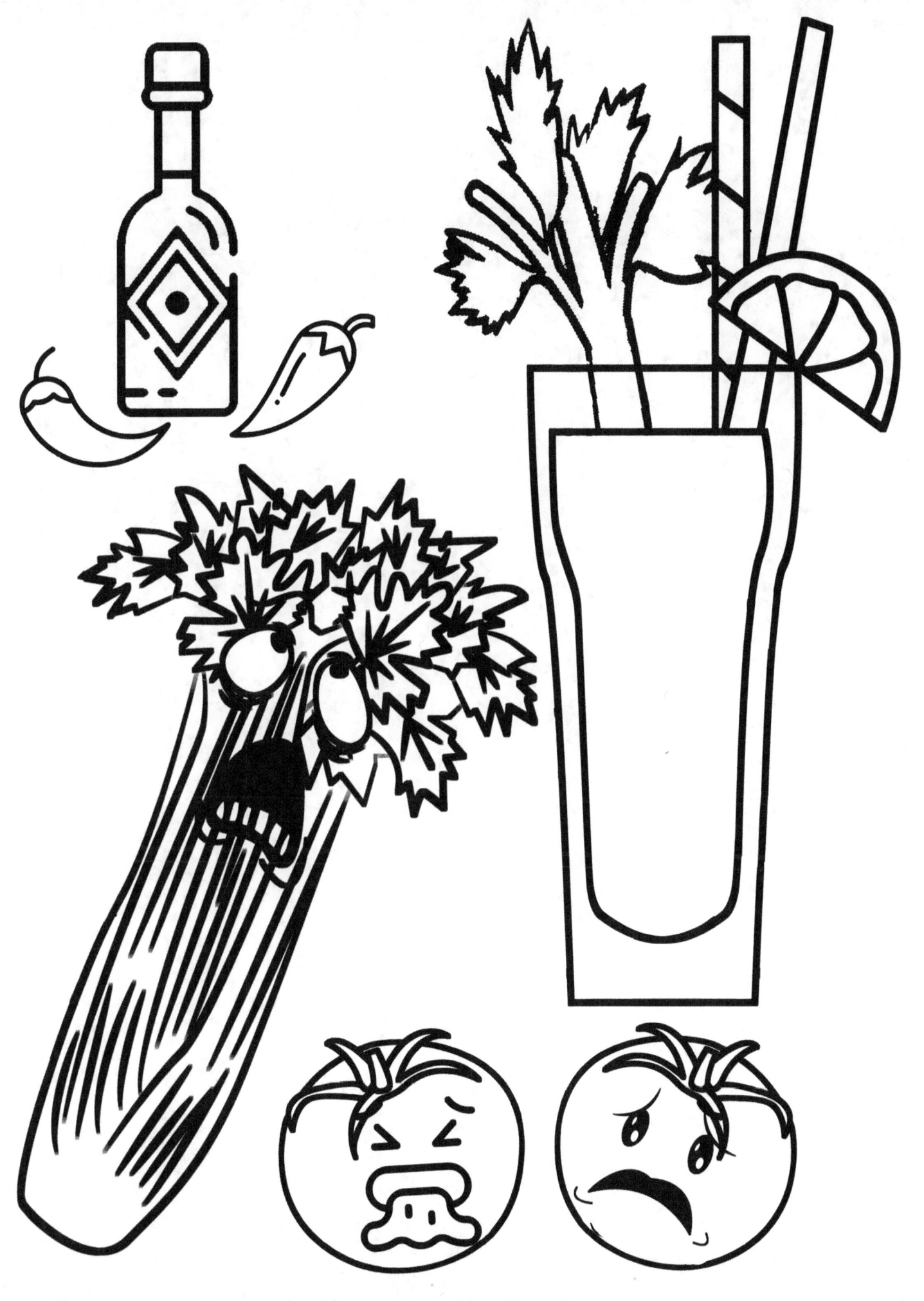

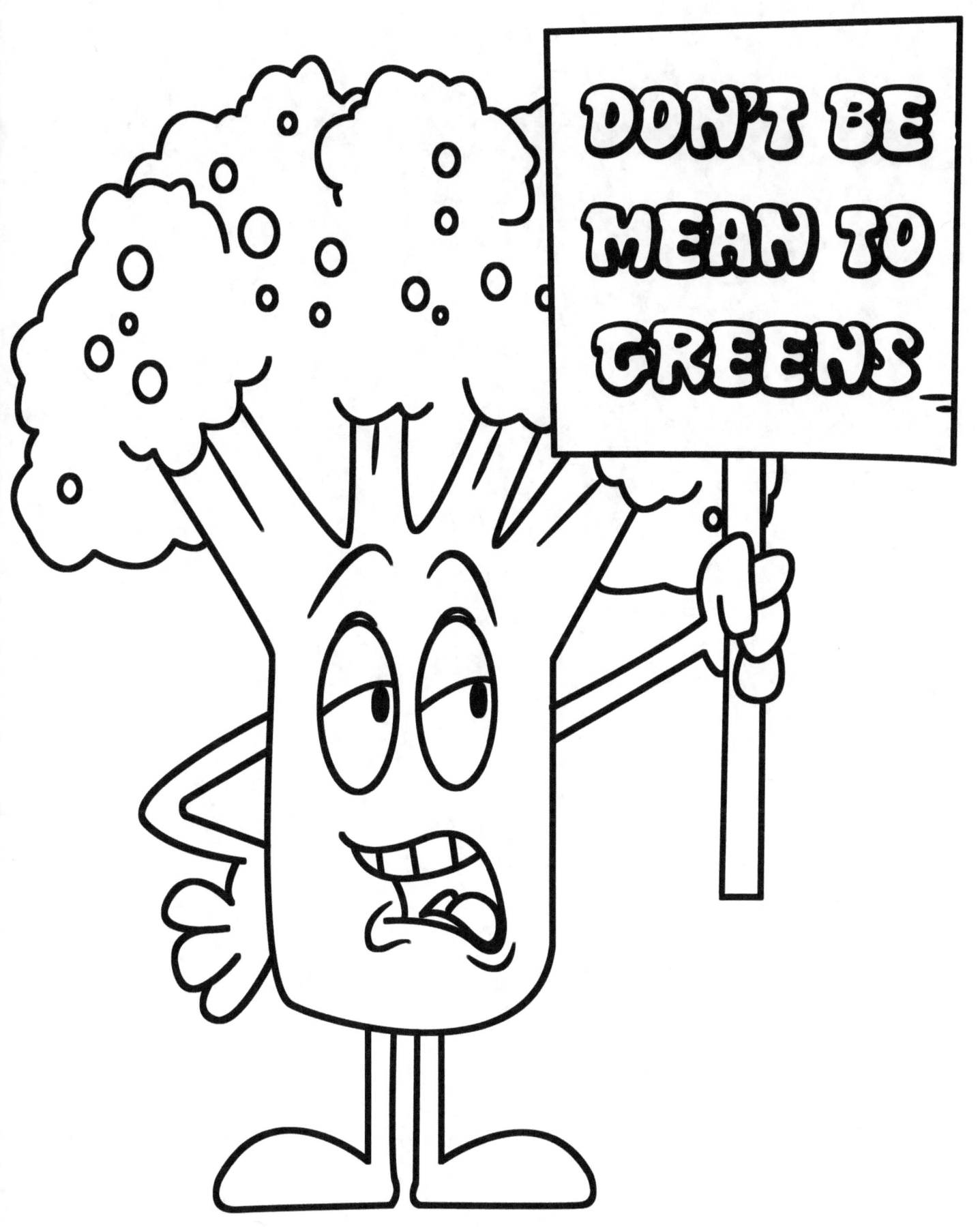

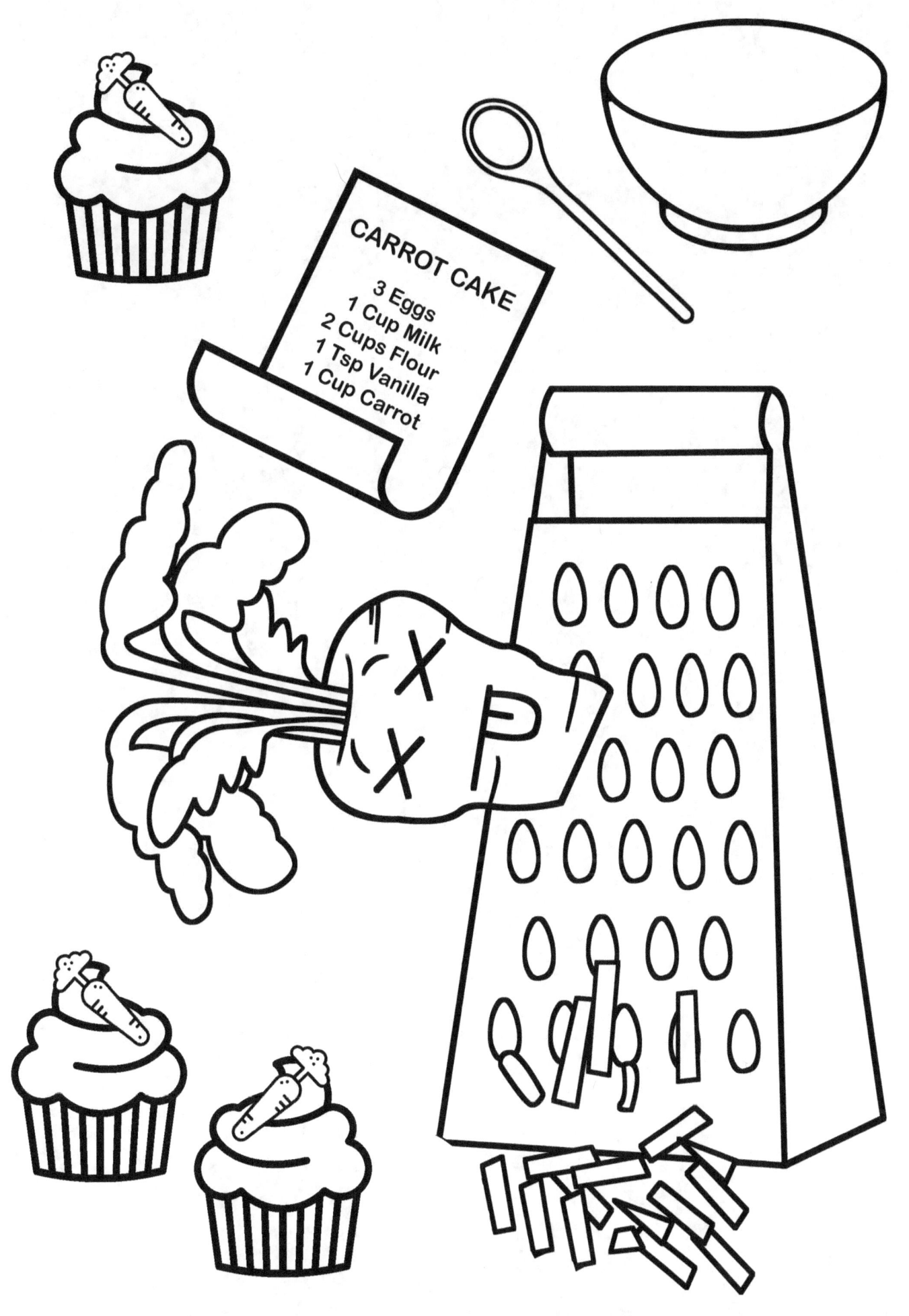

CARROT CAKE

3 Eggs
1 Cup Milk
2 Cups Flour
1 Tsp Vanilla
1 Cup Carrot

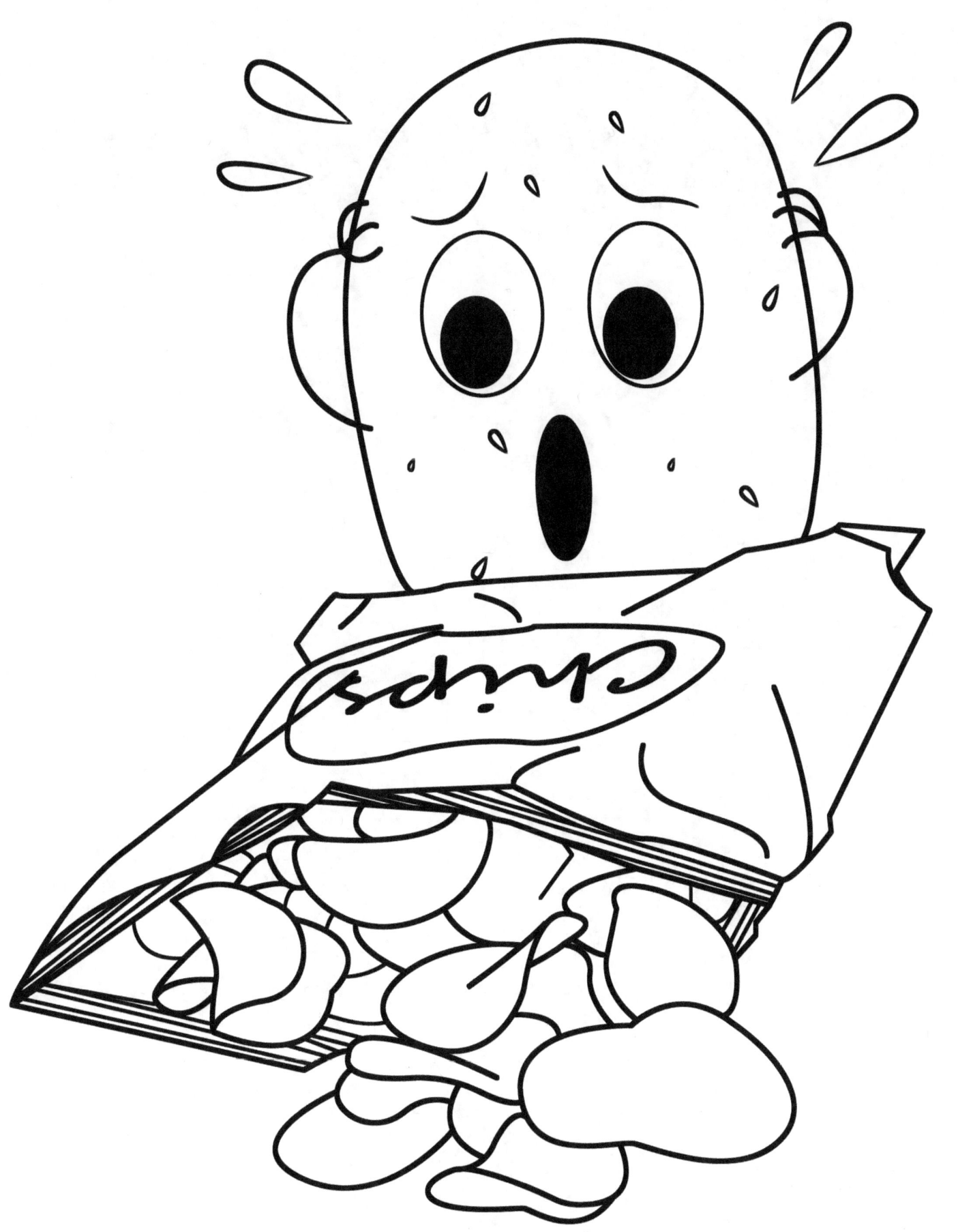

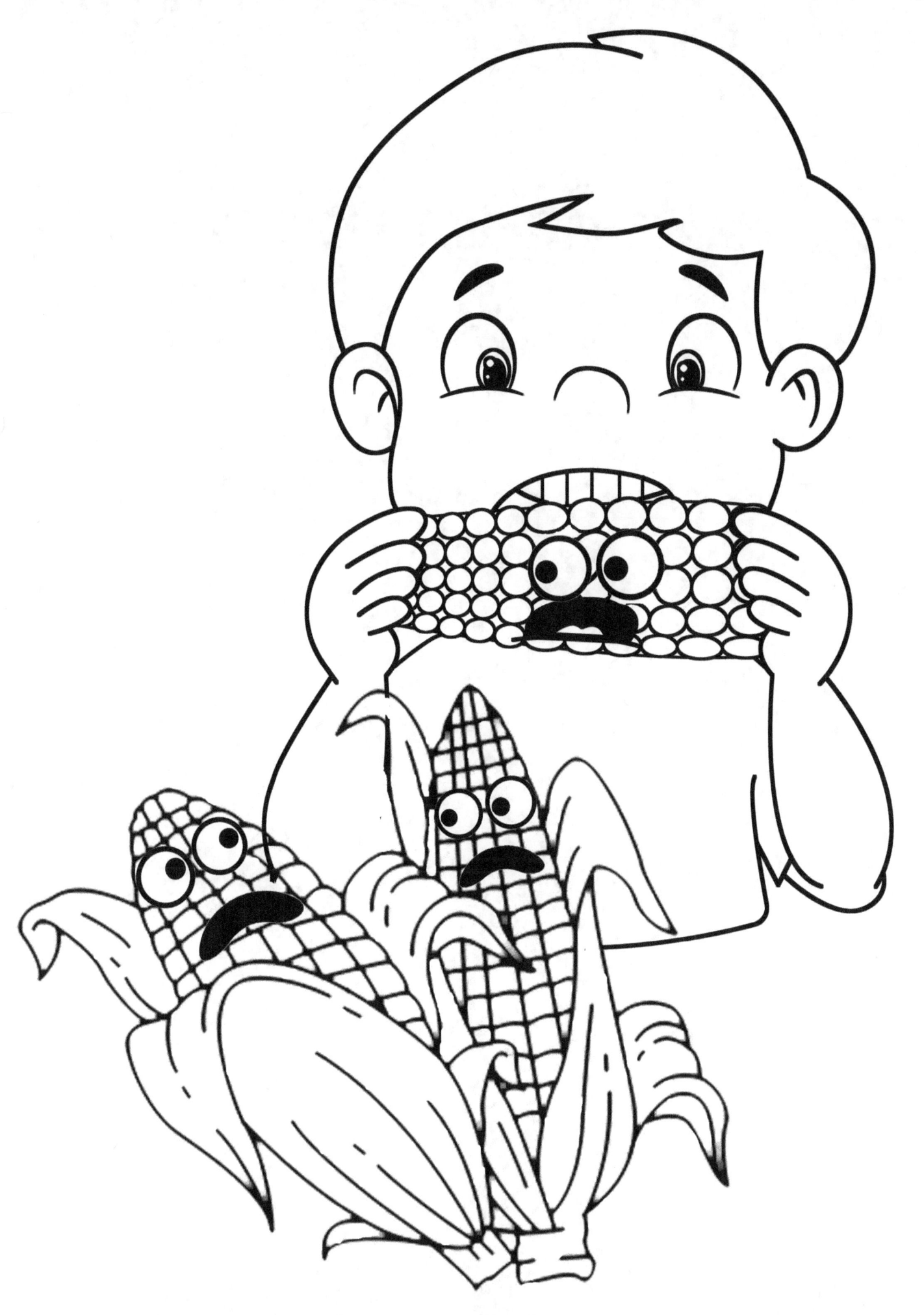

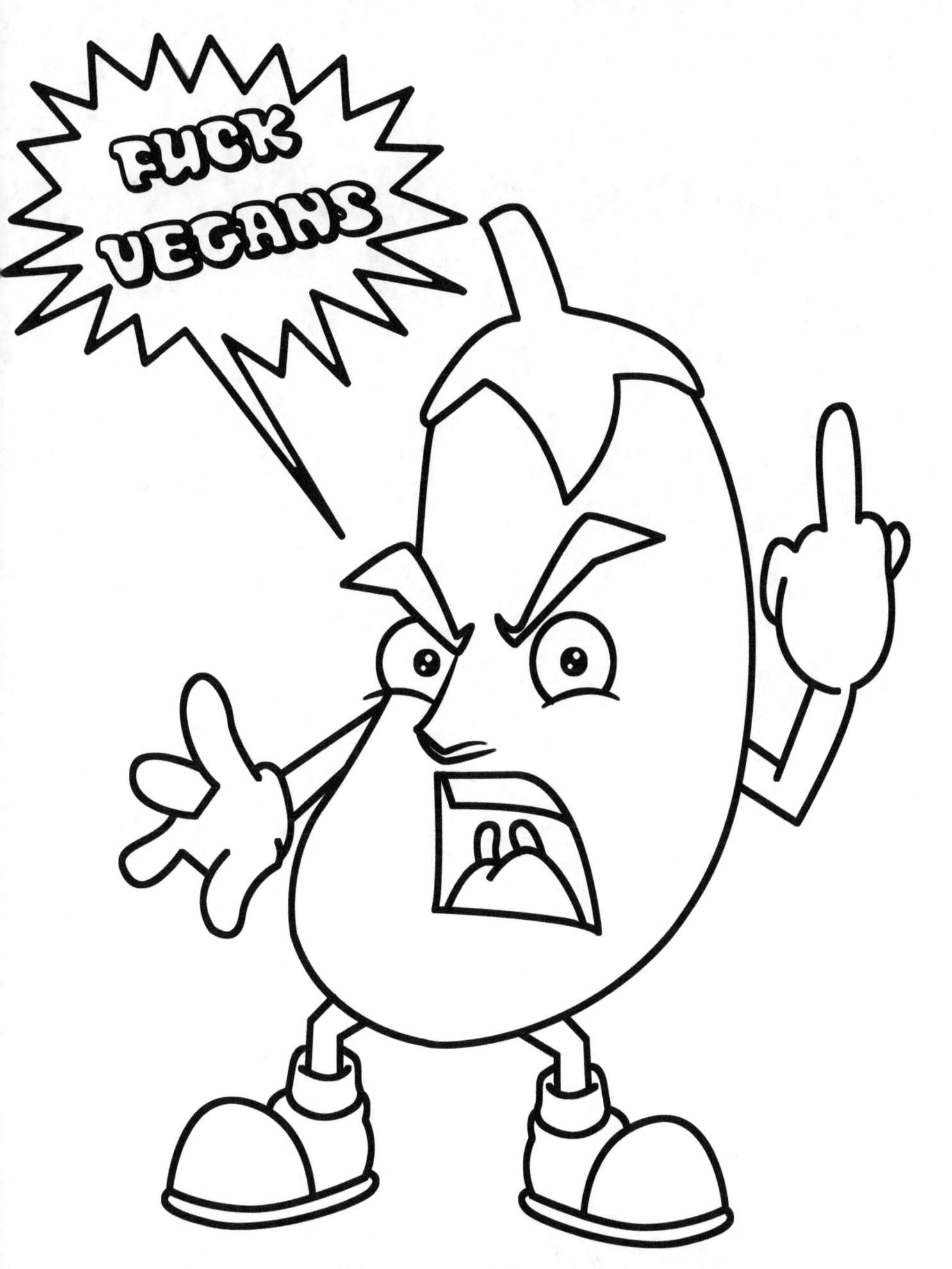

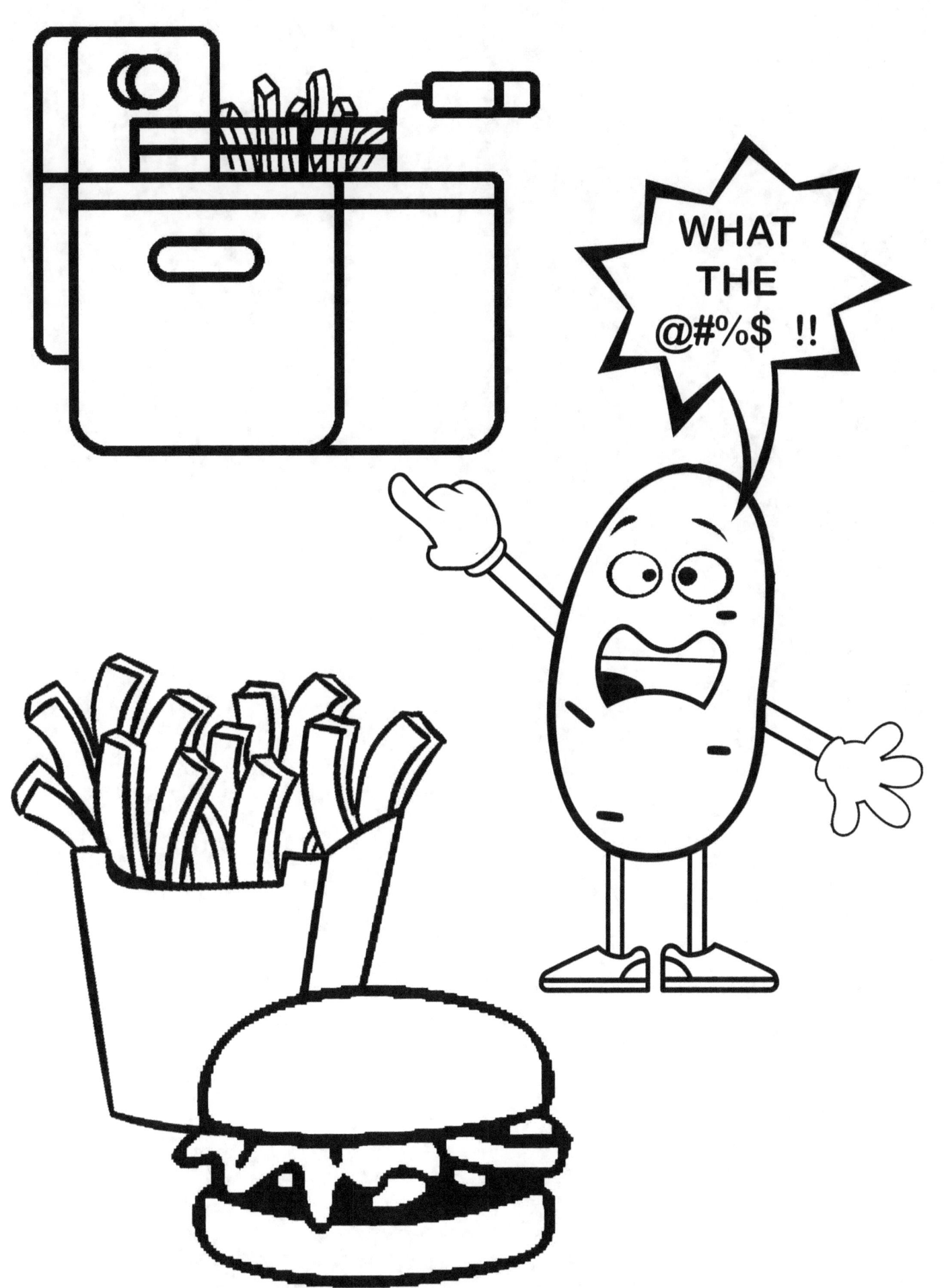

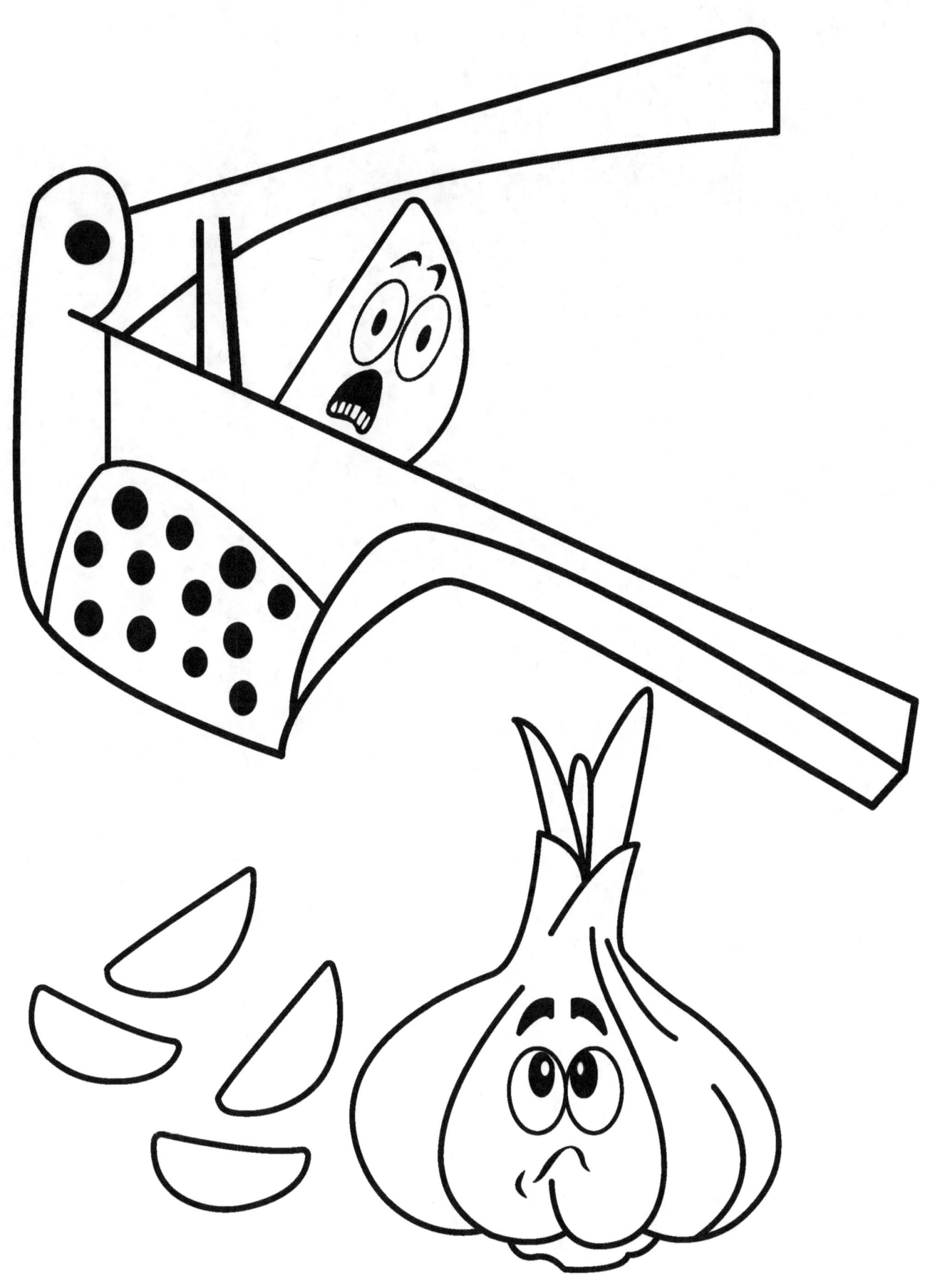

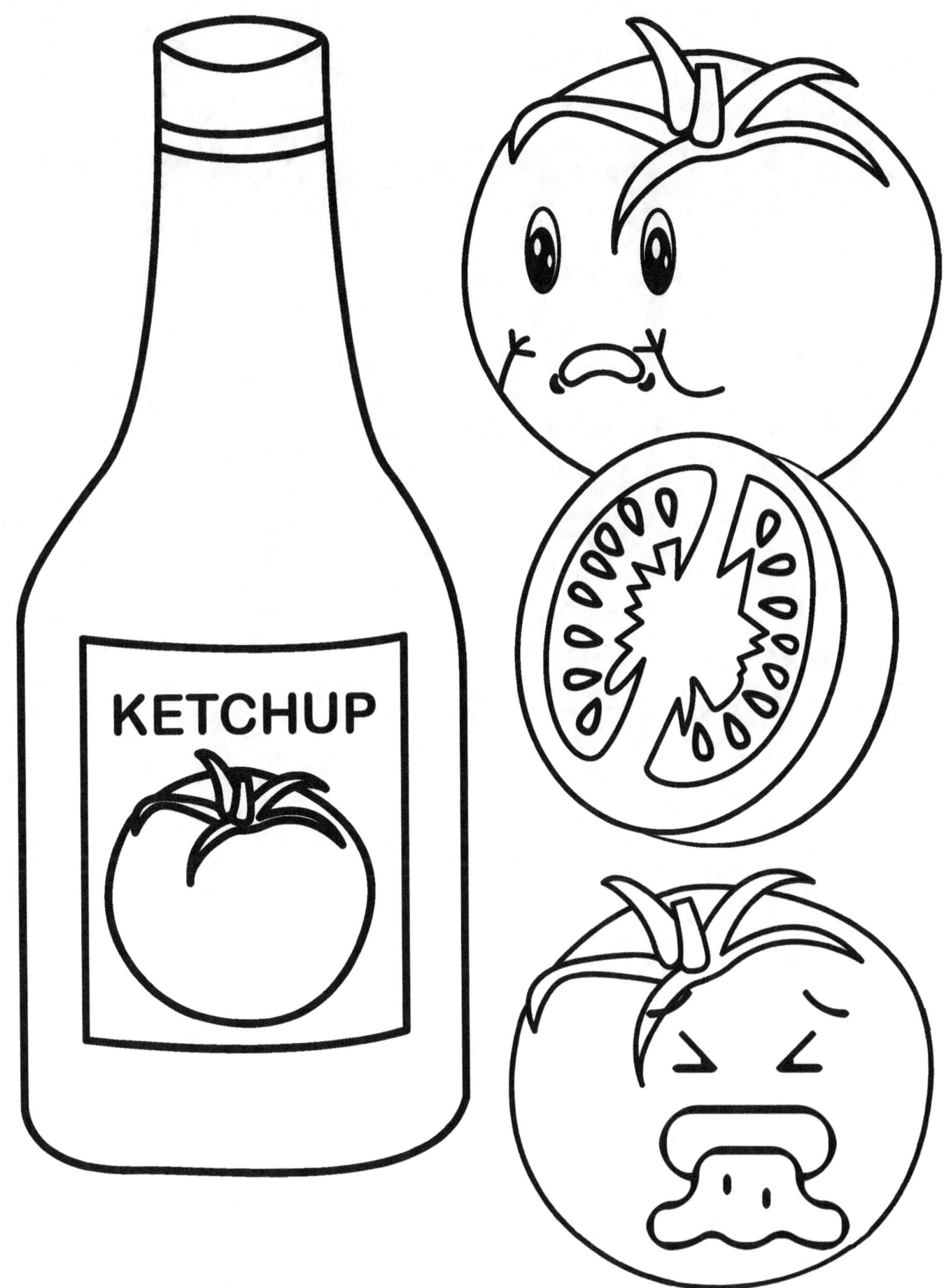

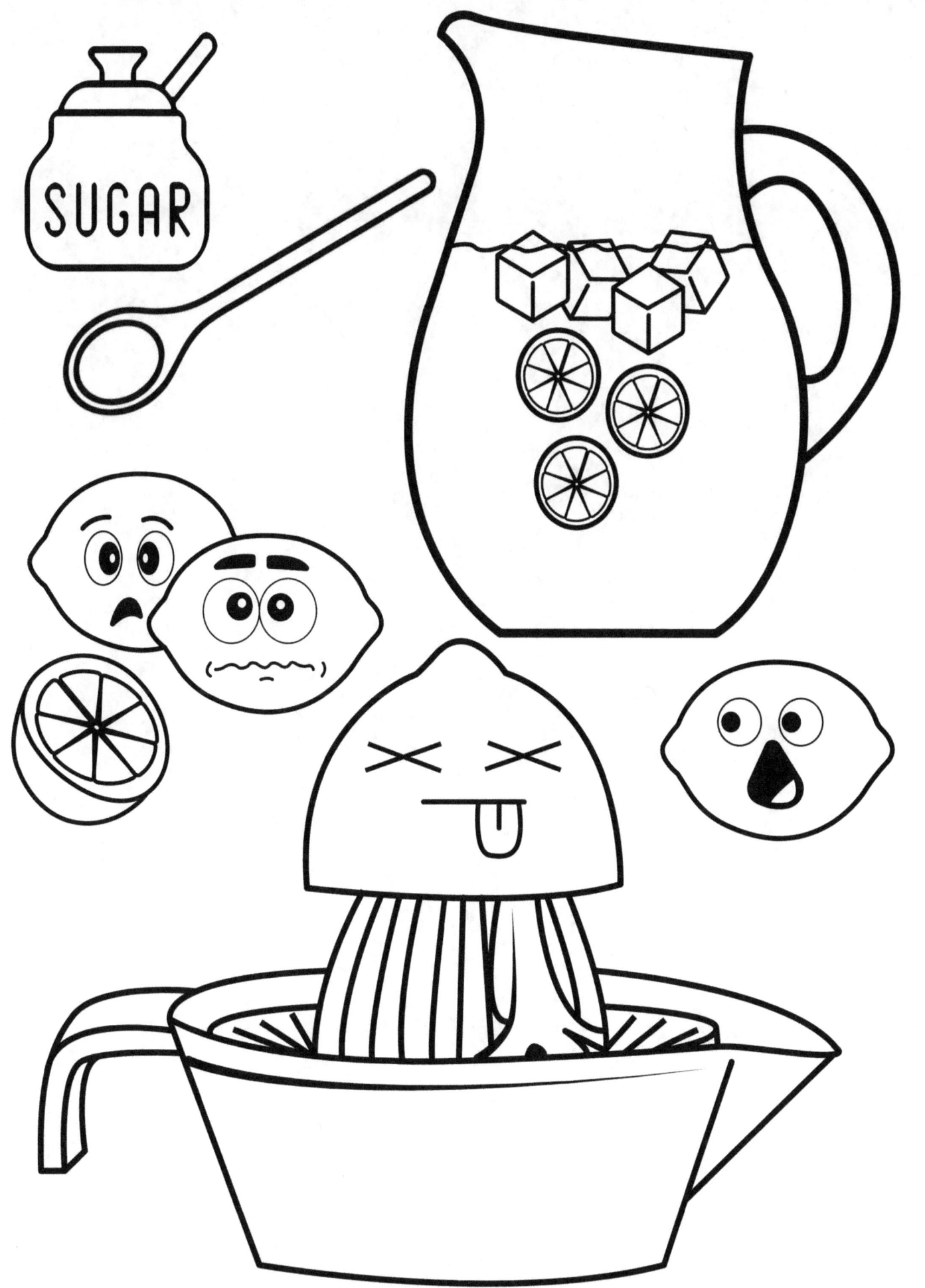

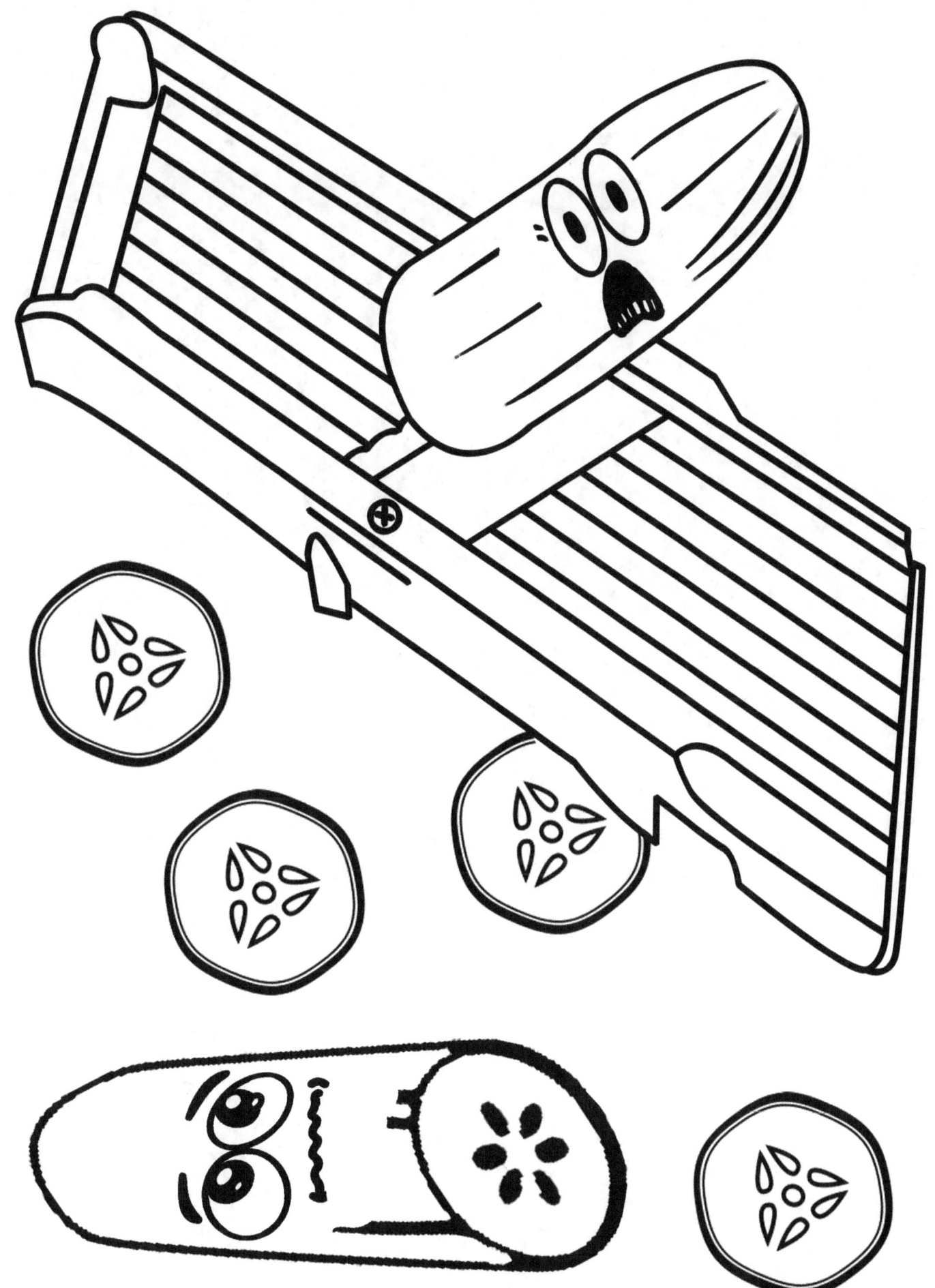

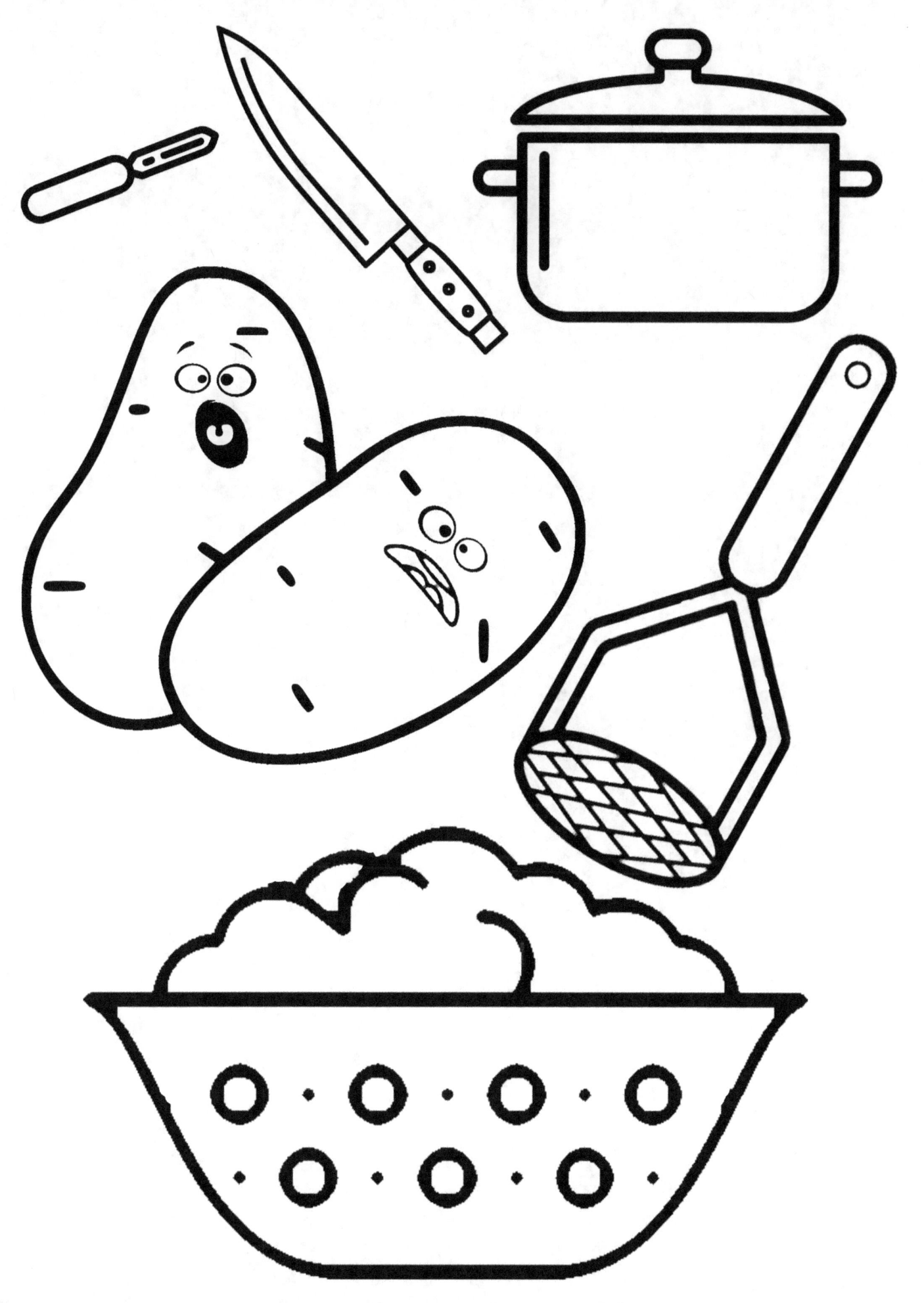

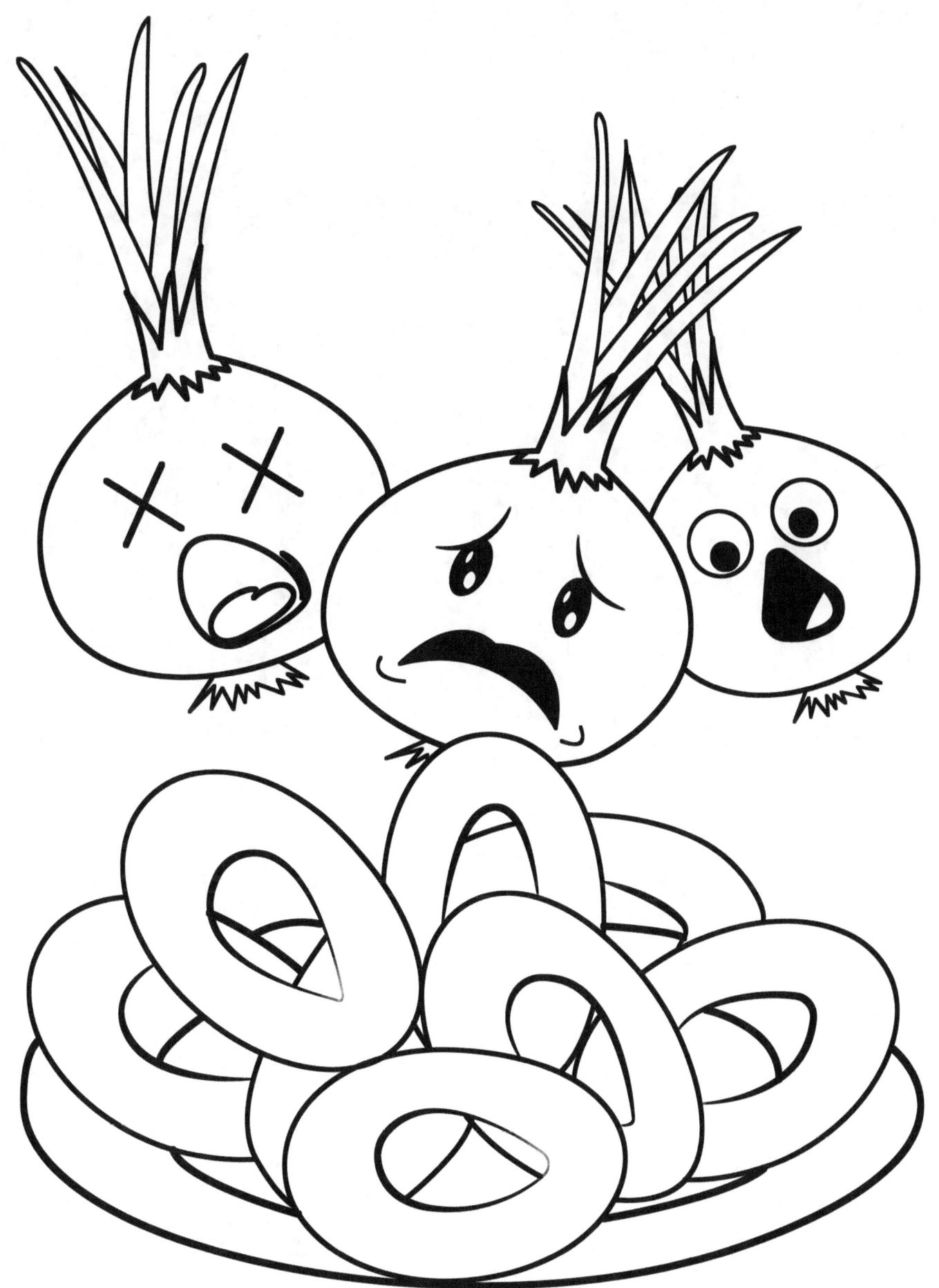

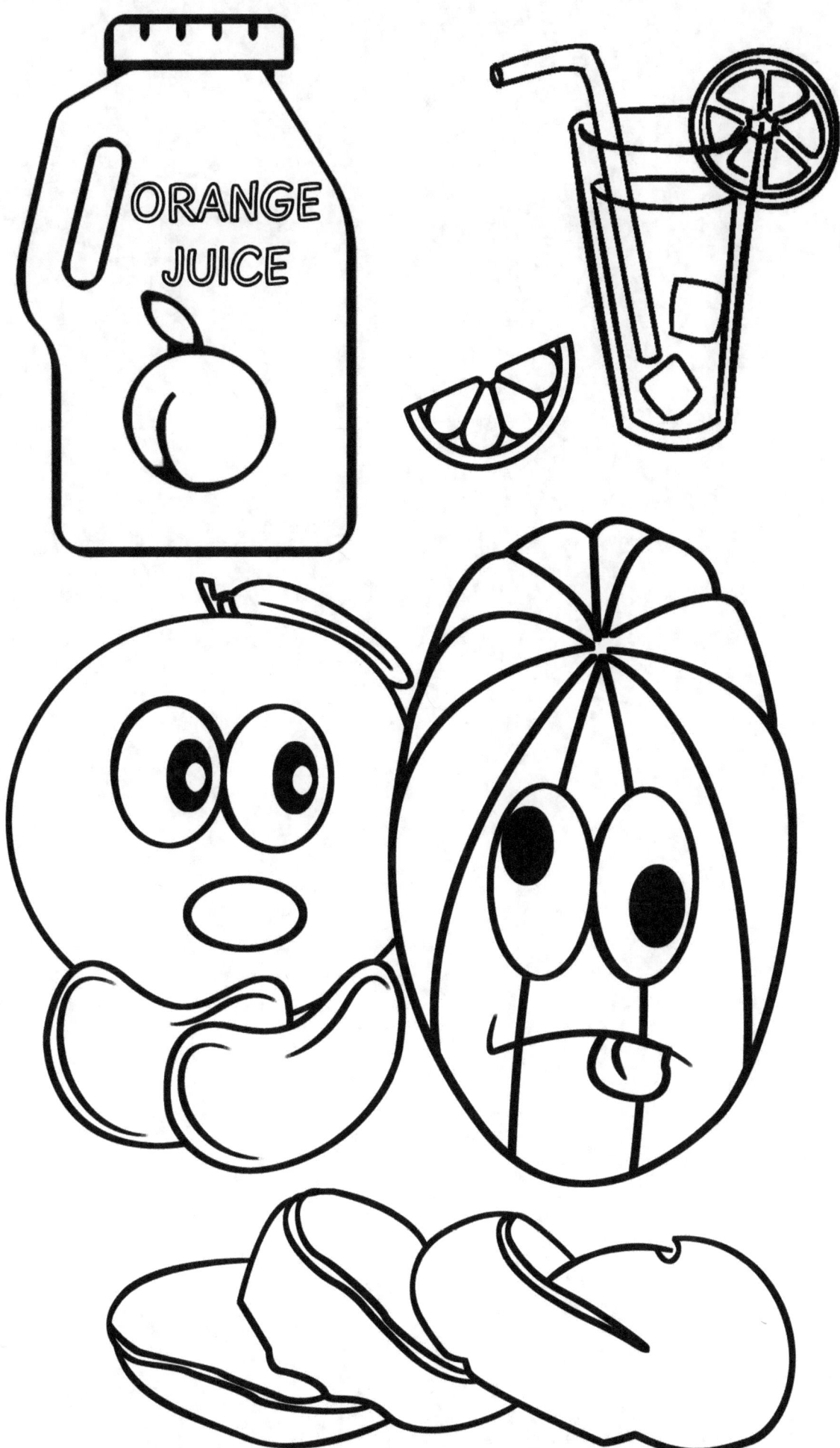

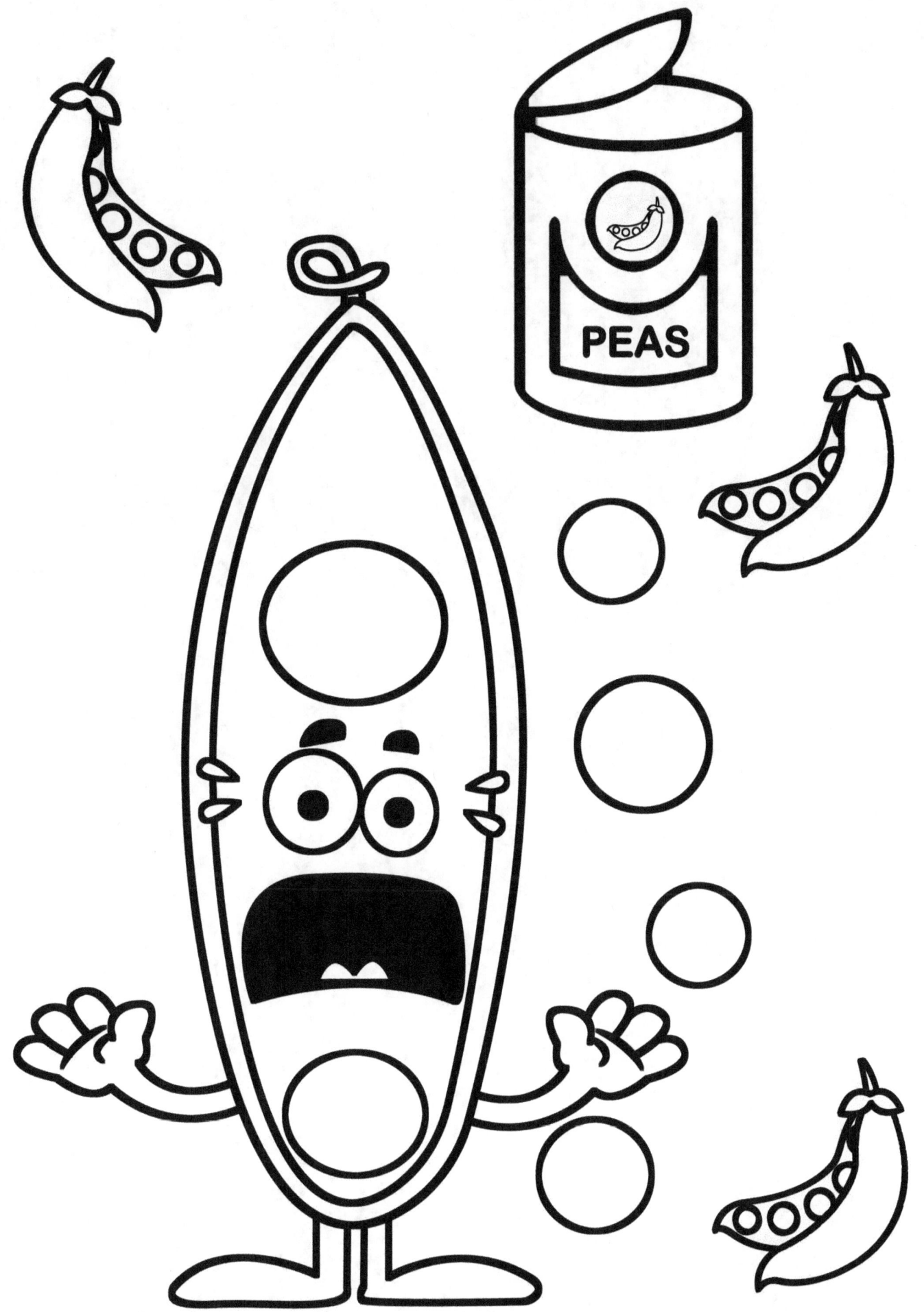

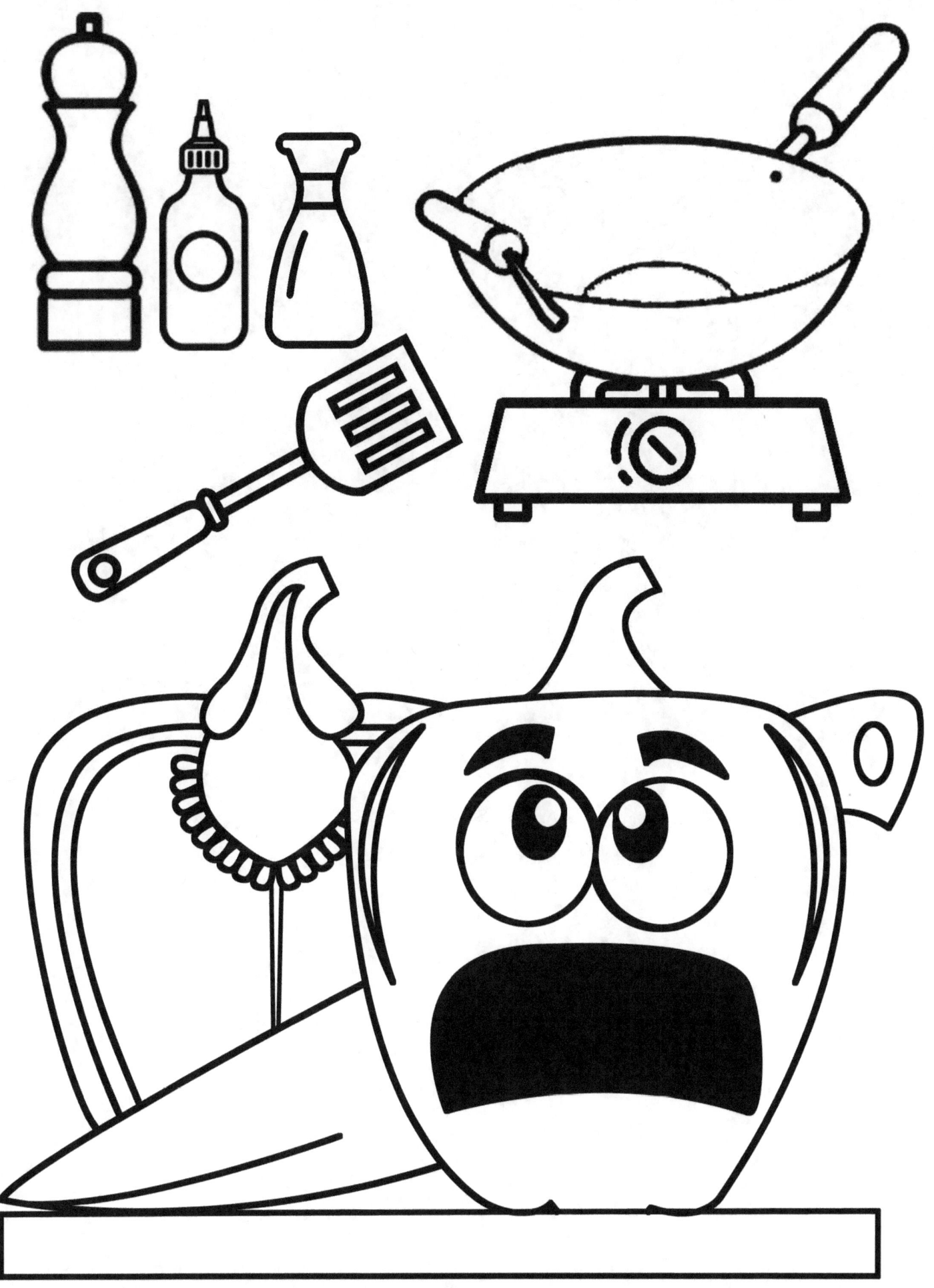

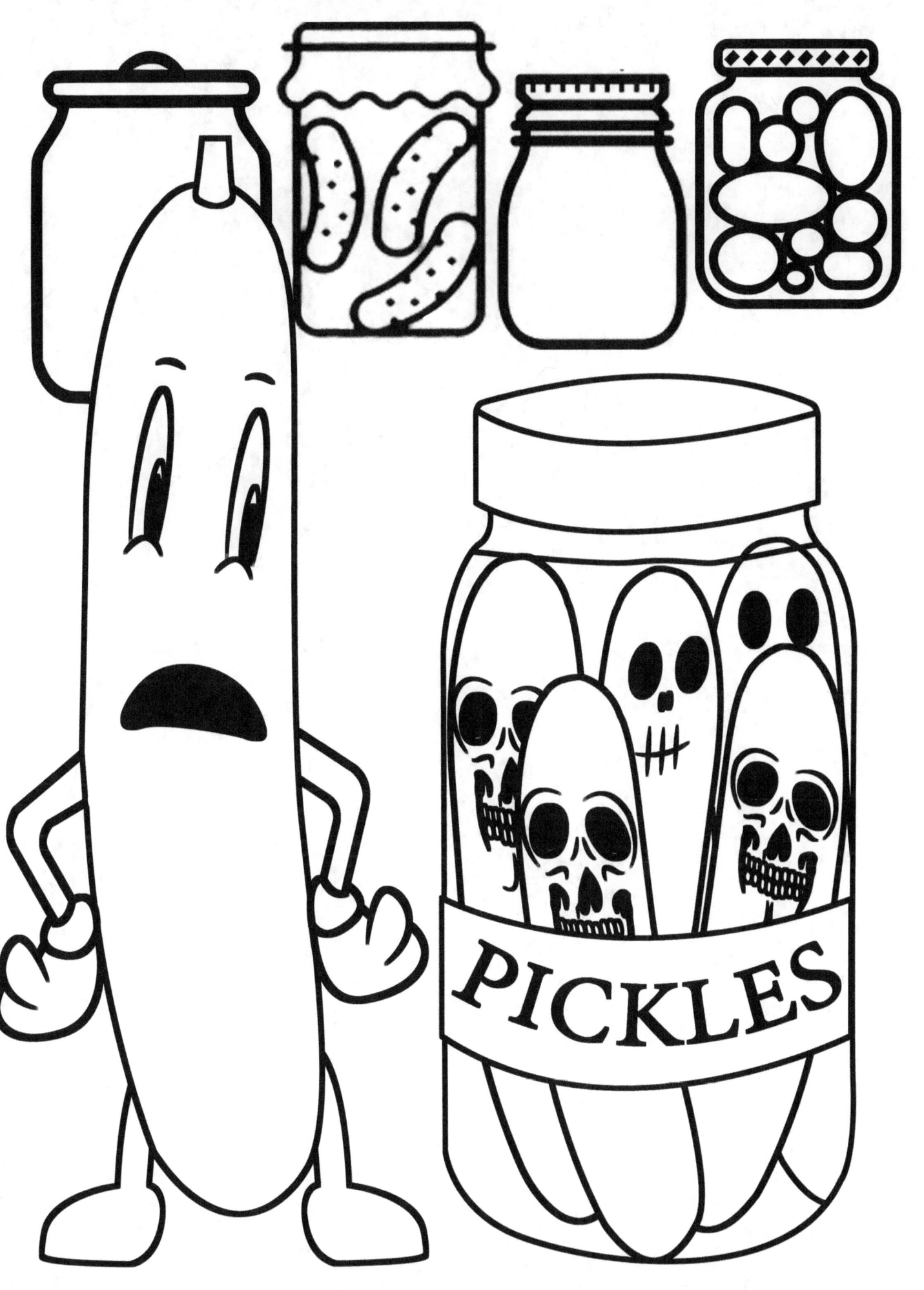

PICKLES

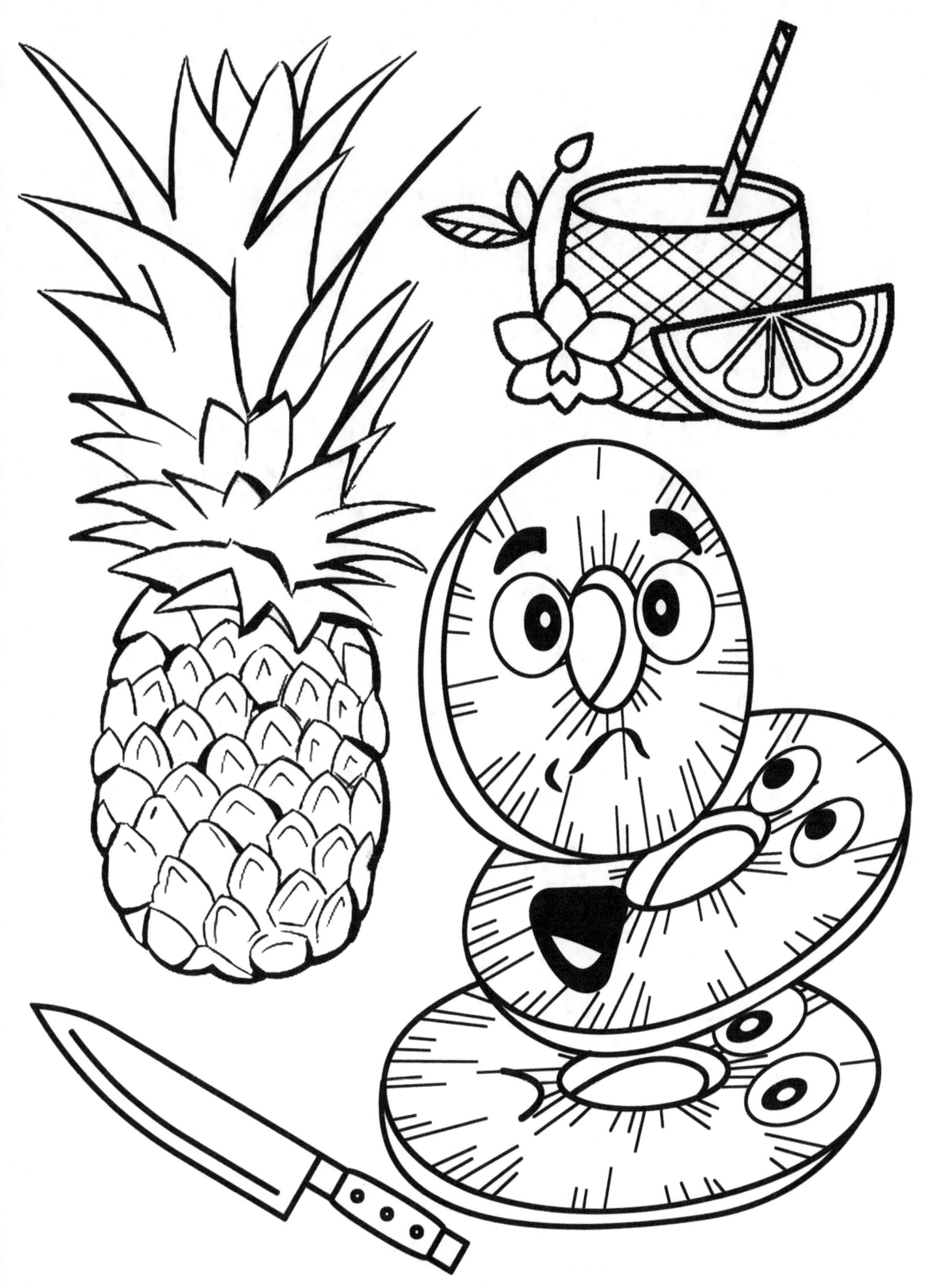

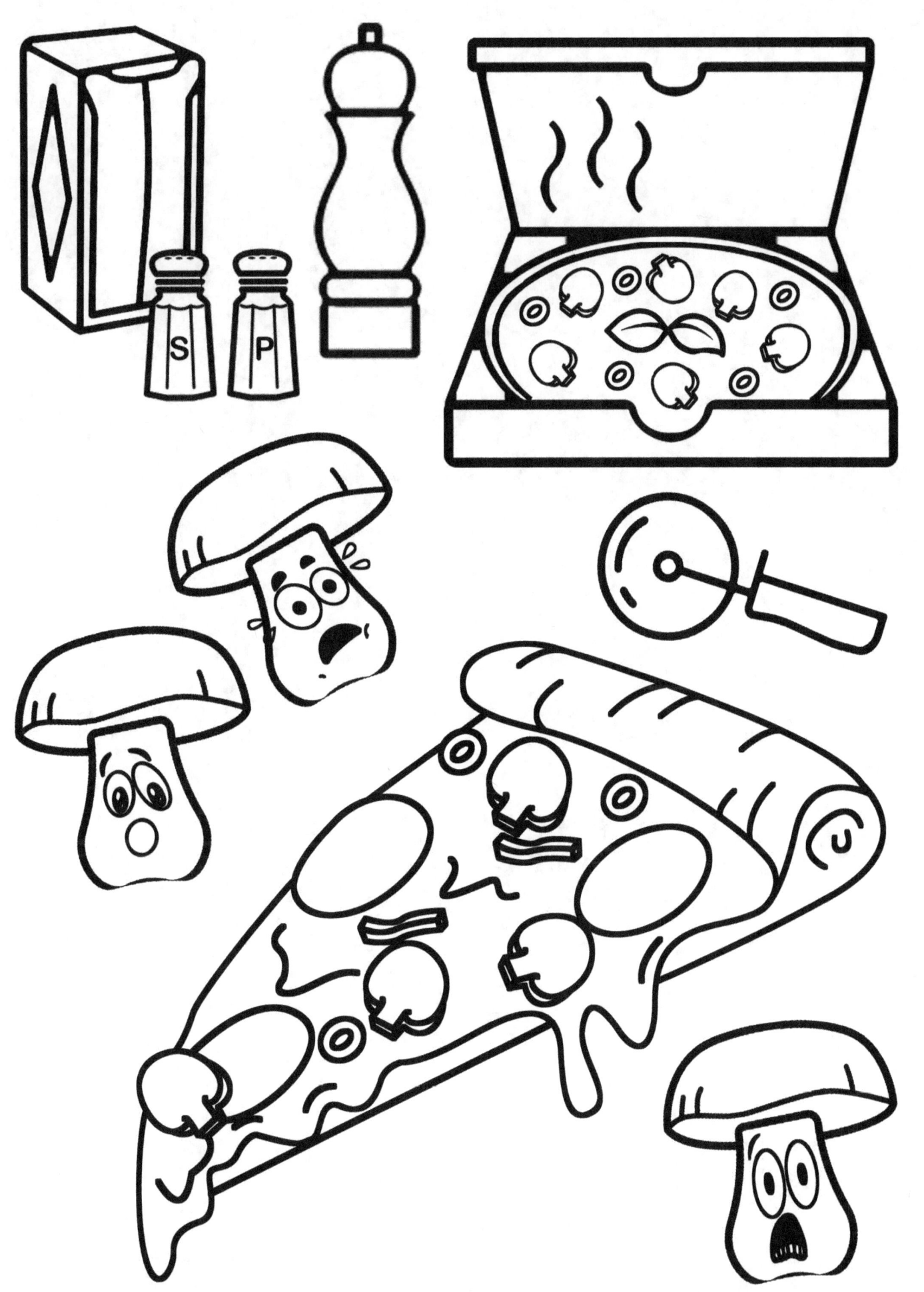

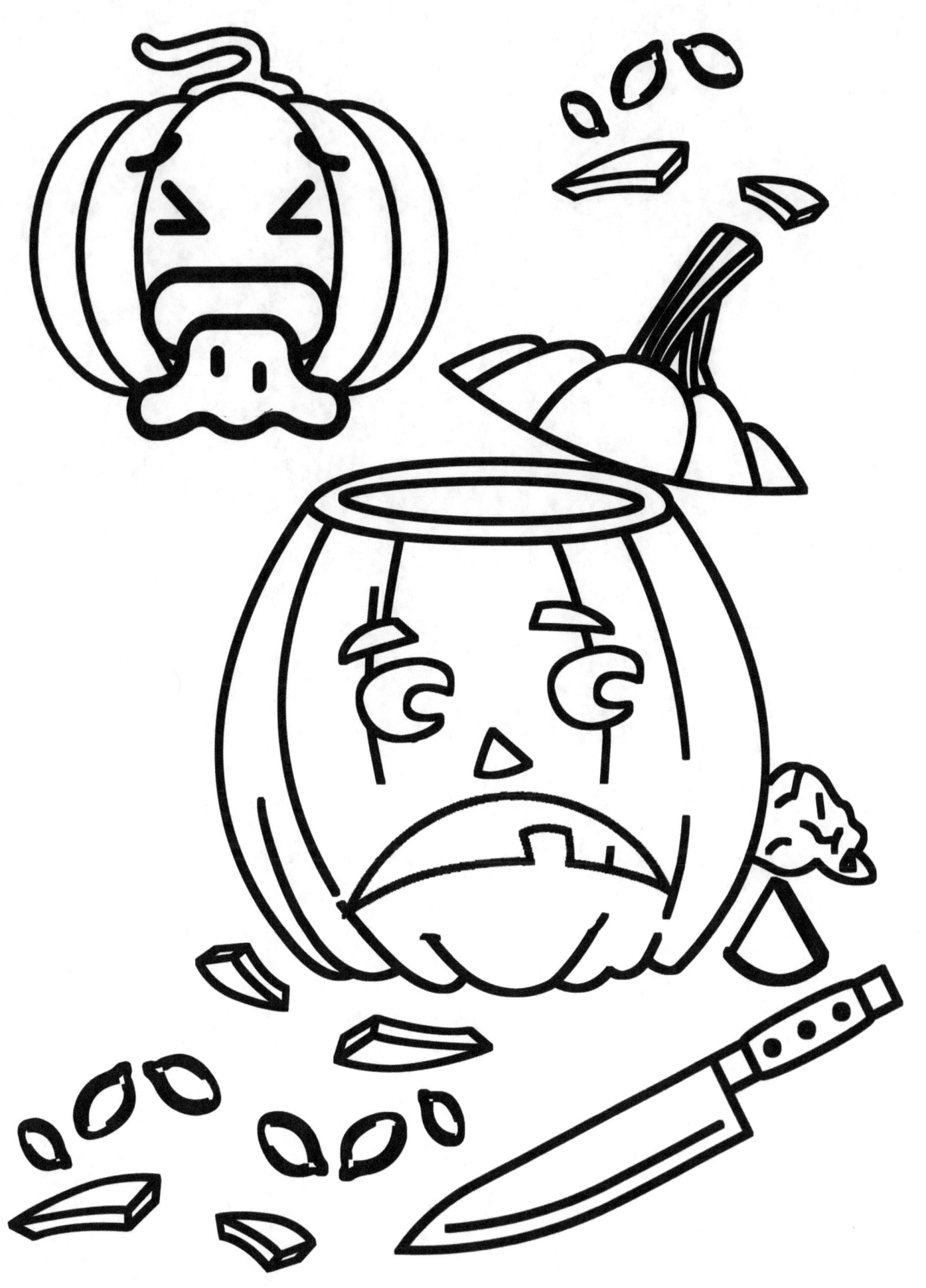

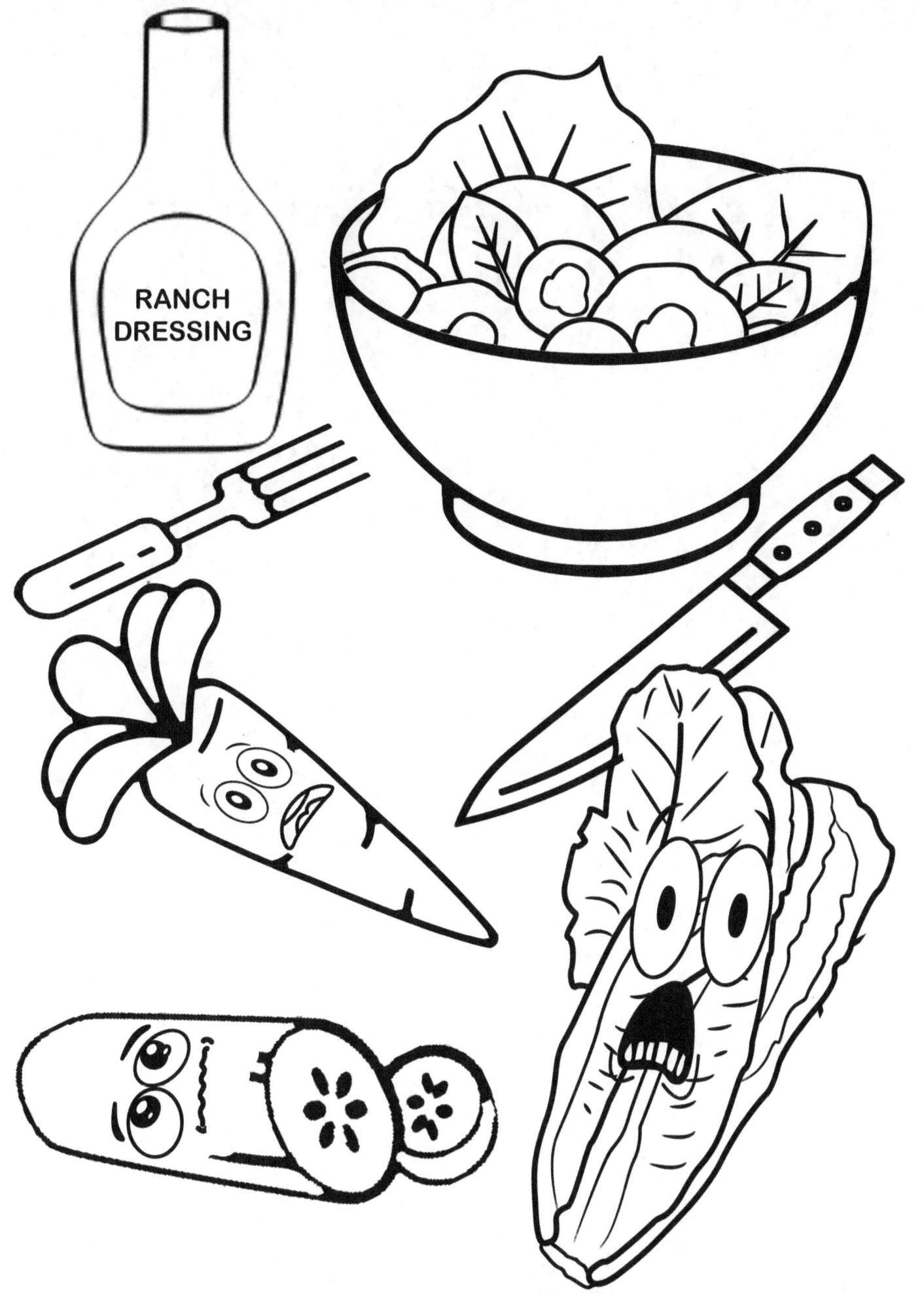

RANCH DRESSING

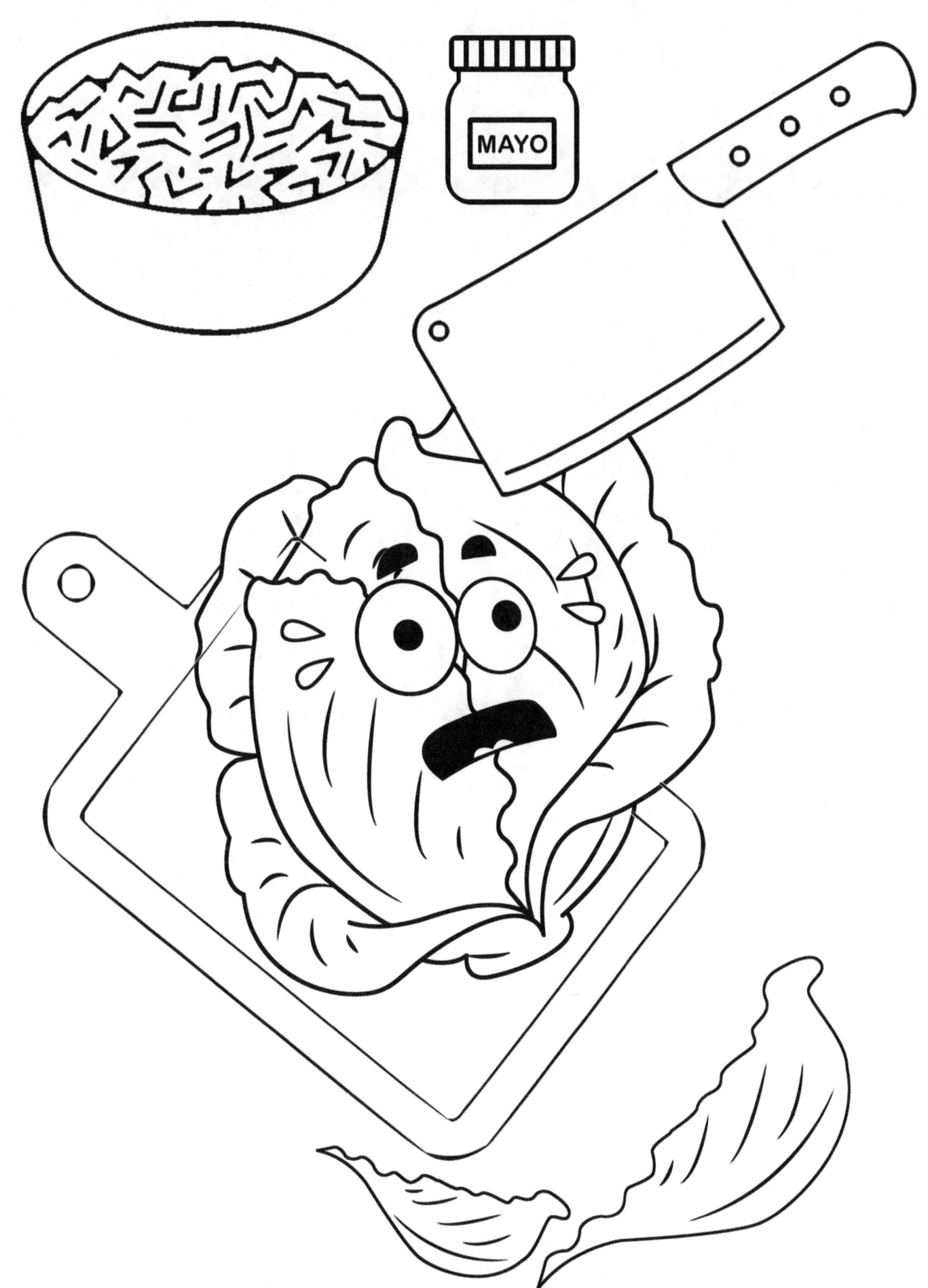

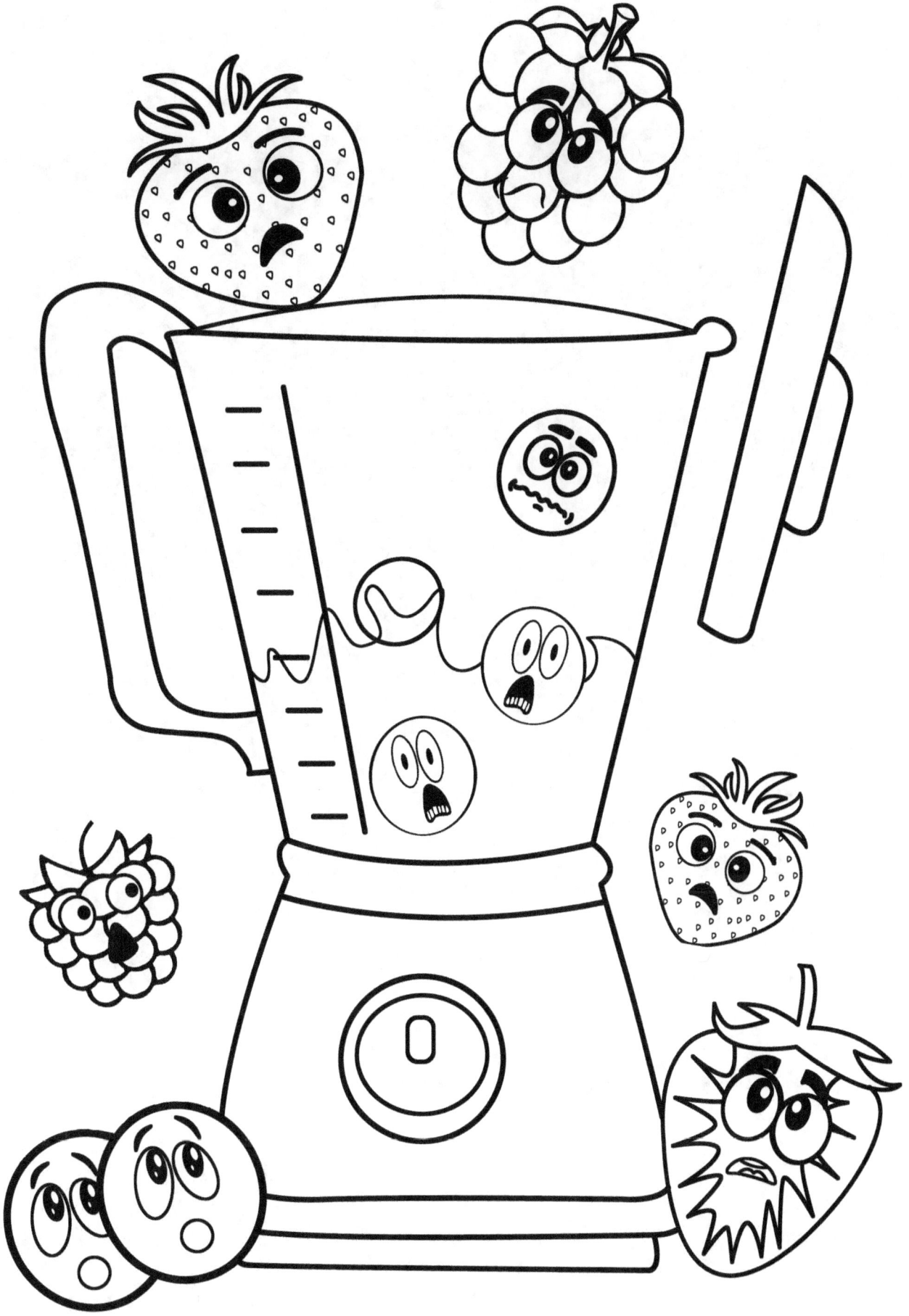

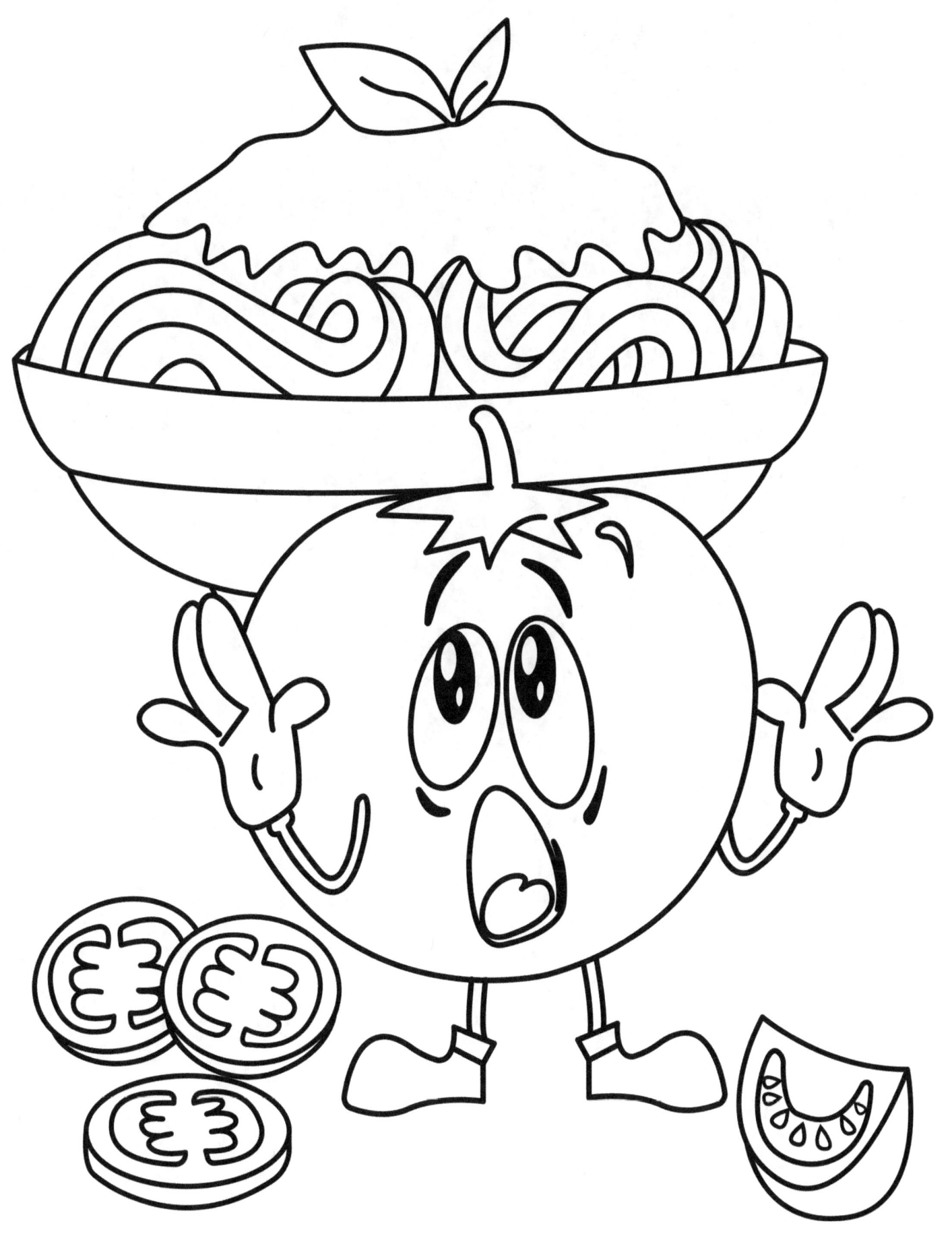

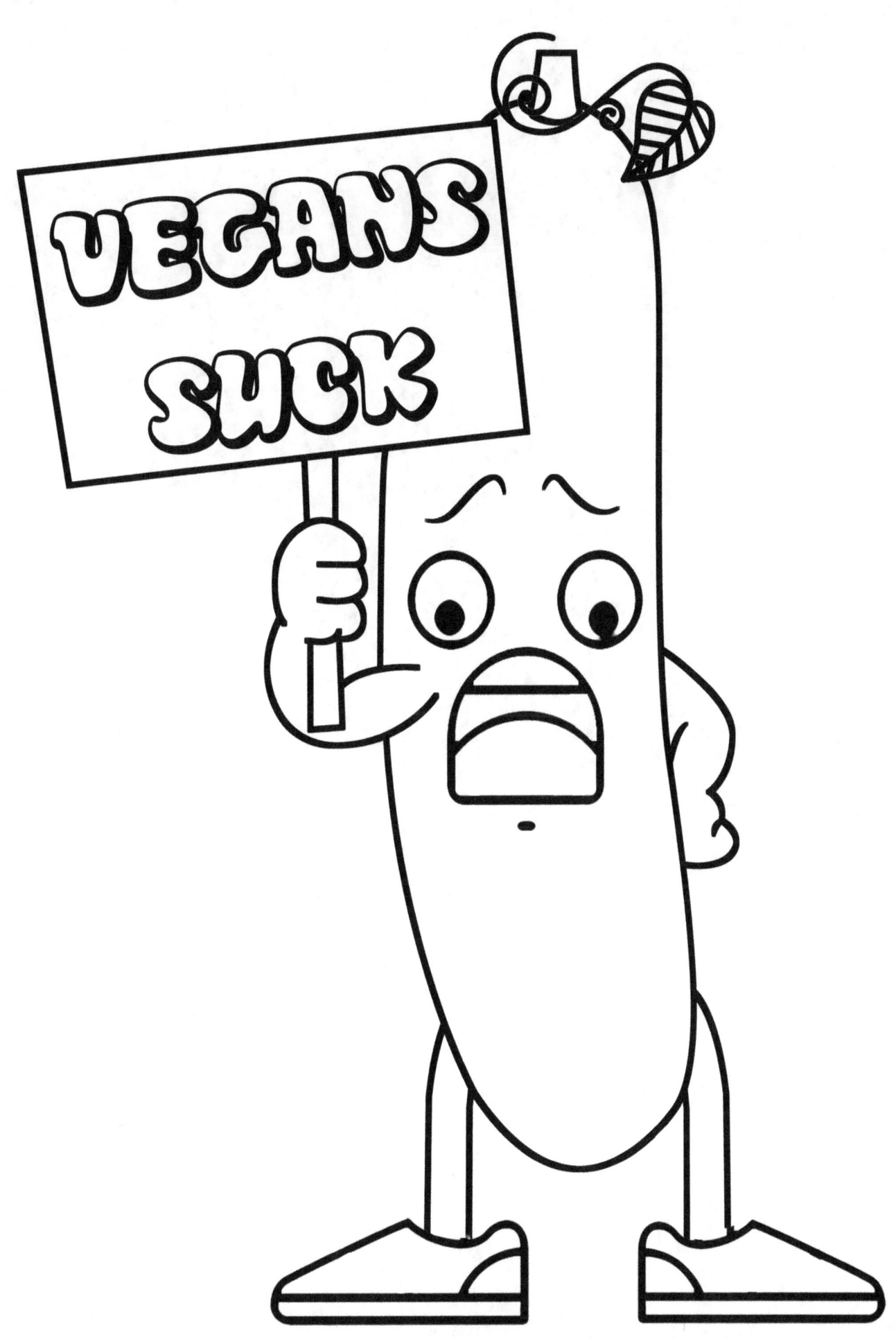

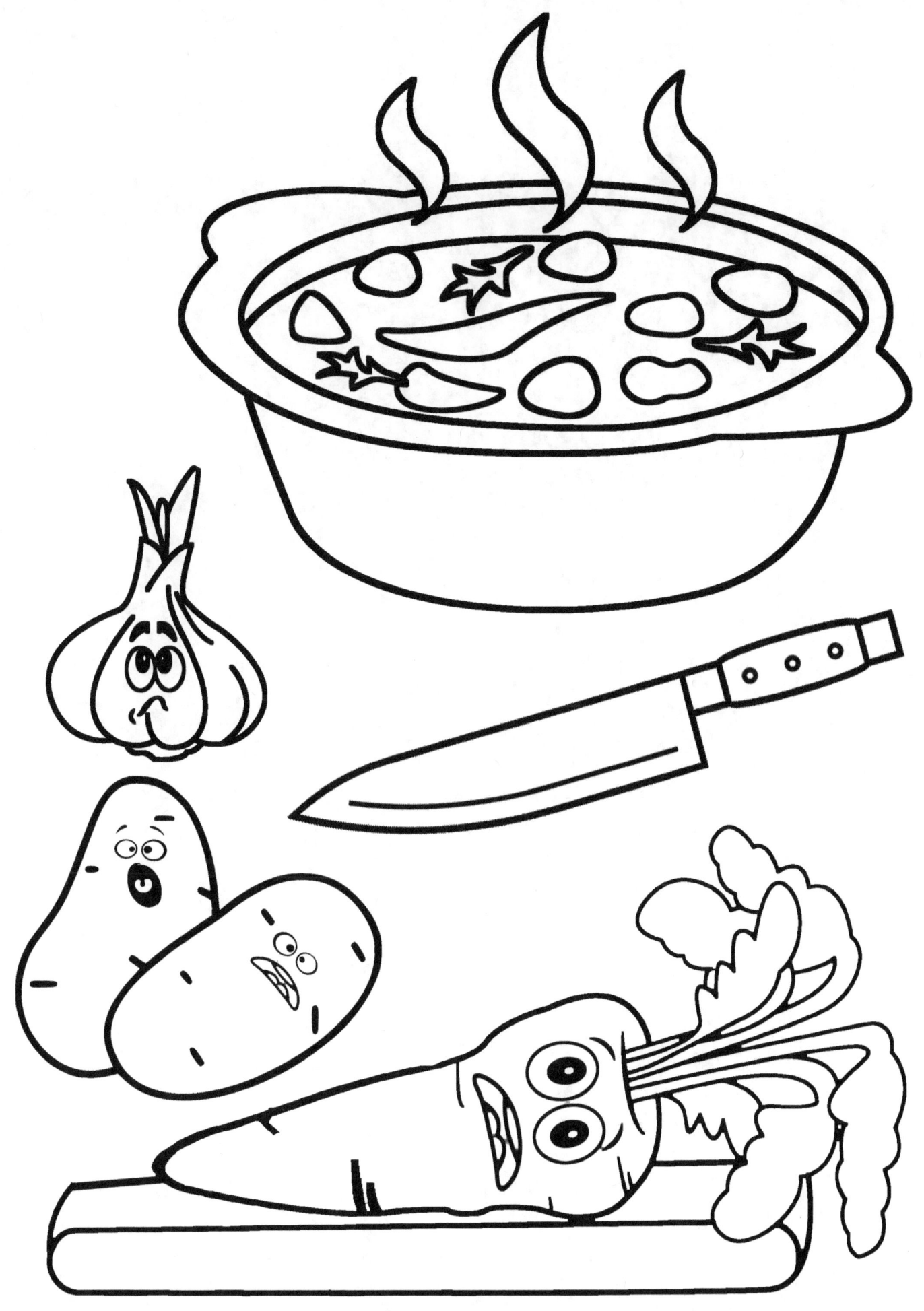

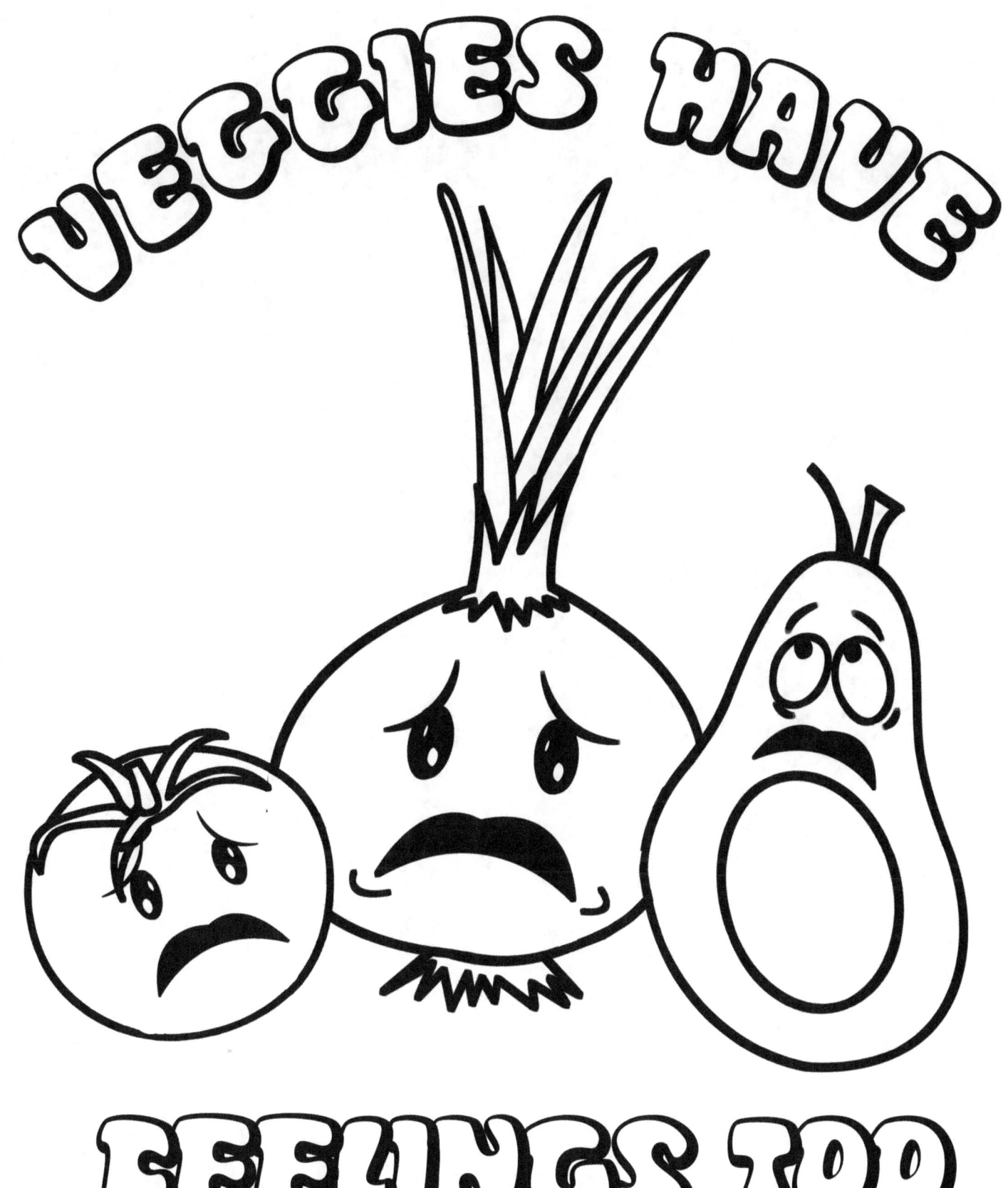

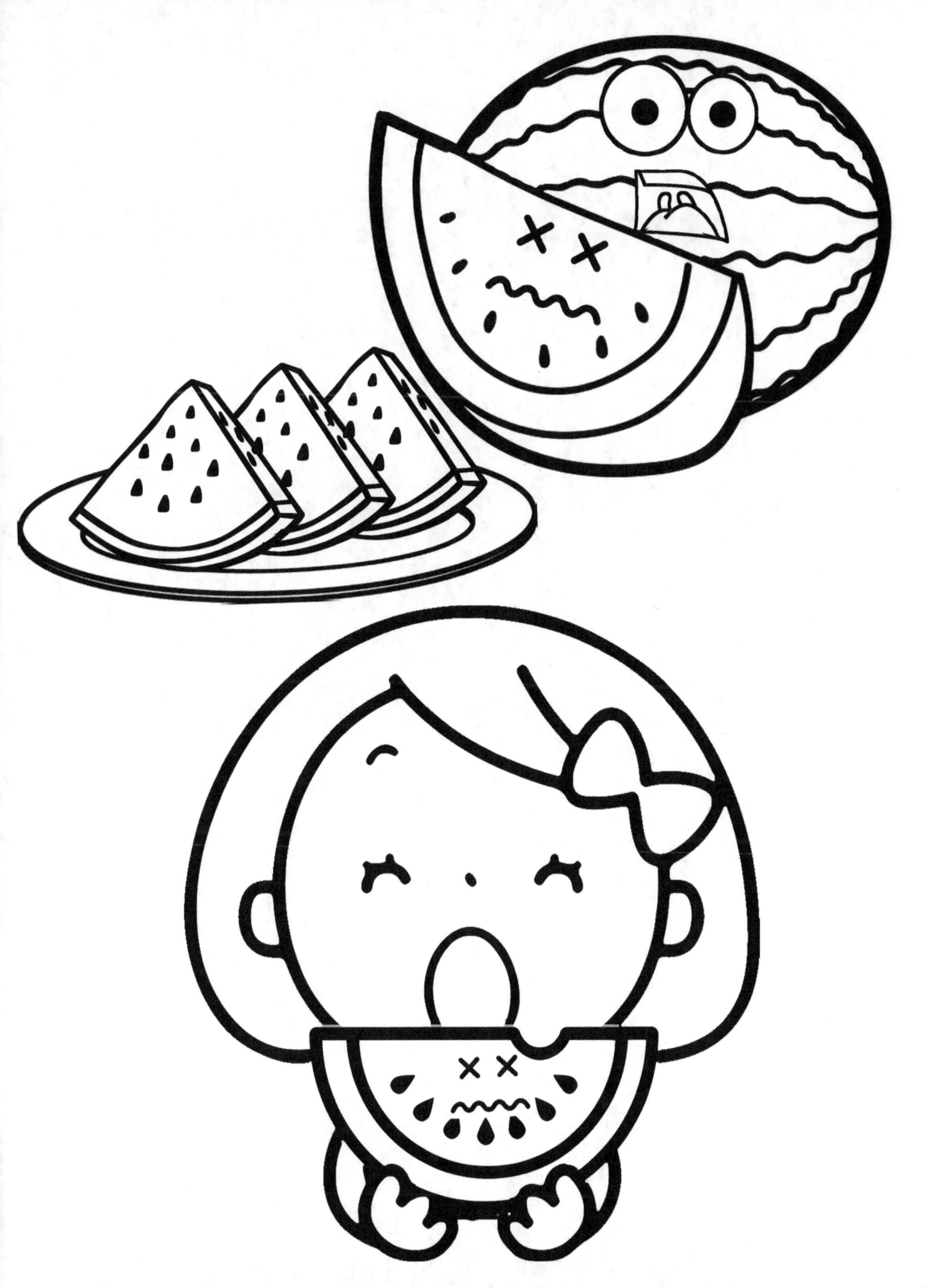

www.ingramcontent.com/pod-product-compliance
Lightning Source LLC
Chambersburg PA
CBHW080902220526
45467CB00008B/2606